THE
COMPLETE CROCHET
HANDBOOK

THE
COMPLETE CROCHET HANDBOOK

Includes everything you need from first steps to finishing

Jane Crowfoot

SEARCH PRESS

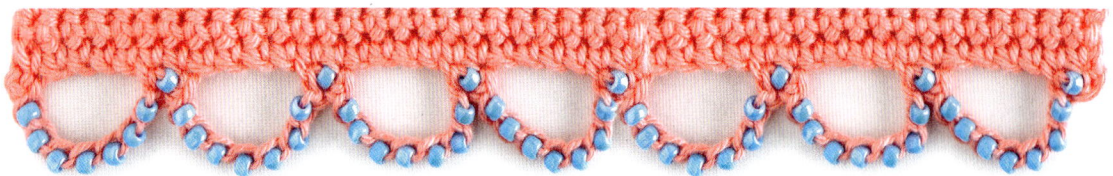

This edition published in 2024 by
Search Press Ltd
Wellwood North Farm Road
Tunbridge Wells
Kent TN2 3DR

ISBN 978-1-8009-2241-9
Ebook ISBN 978-1-8009-3228-9

Bookmarked Hub
For further ideas and inspiration, and to join our free online
community, visit www.bookmarkedhub.com

Conceived, edited and designed by
Quarto Publishing, an imprint of Quarto
1 Triptych Place
London
SE1 9SH
www.quarto.com

QUAR: 1170394

Editor: Claire Waite Brown
Managing editor: Lesley Henderson
Proofreader: Jane Roe
Designer: Sally Bond
Art director Martina Calvio
Photographer: Phil Wilkins
Additional photography: Leanne Jade
Illustrator: Kuo Kang Chen
Publisher: Lorraine Dickey

Printed in China

MIX
Paper | Supporting
responsible forestry
FSC® C016973

Contents

Meet Jane!

As a child I remember watching my great grandmother, Alice, arranging crocheted granny squares on her lap and making decisions about colour combinations. When she was young Alice was no doubt taught to make delicate crochet items such as doilies and lace-style edgings, using very fine yarns and tiny hooks, but it was in the 1960s, when she was well into her seventies, that she fell in love with making granny squares and the creative opportunity they provided.

My great-aunt Kit, Alice's daughter, told me once that Alice 'simply loved yarn', and that she would spend hours working out her vibrant designs. Her speedy hook and agile fingers fascinated me, and her love for fibre certainly rubbed off on me. However, it wasn't until much later in my life that I also found myself enthralled by, and addicted to, the art of crochet.

I completed a degree in Textile Design in my early twenties, and went on to work within the craft industry teaching knitting workshops and providing technical demonstrations. By 2005, as crochet started to feature more frequently in contemporary books and magazines, I found myself drawn to the craft once again, and wanted to learn to make something more complicated than granny squares and simple edgings. My crochet knowledge at this time was rudimentary, but I was spurred on by a strong desire to design my own crochet fabrics.

I am passionate about designing for the home interior rather than for garments, and I love how well crochet adapts itself to this. As a lover of surface pattern, I can add so many design aspects to items for the home, without having to think about how these features would look on the contours of a body. I think of my designs as pieces of artwork, and I especially like creating borders and frames that complement them, often throwing in as many stitches and features as I can. Designing items for the home, such as afghans, cushions, and throws, sits well within my conscience. I am not producing items for fast fashion, and putting my patterns out in the marketplace in the way that I do, with no obligation to source specific yarns or kits, provides makers with the chance to use yarns that best suit them.

Items for the home last for years. We have afghans that were made by my great-grandmother decades ago, and they still look as good as new, so I love the fact that my designs can become heirlooms of the future for families all over the world, in much the same way as Alice's have been passed down through the generations of my family.

I would love to see crochet recognized as a platform for creativity, and so have made it my mission to seek out pathways that will enable me to reach a wide audience to whom I can demonstrate the versatility and integrity of the craft. I try to highlight the differences between 'homemade' and 'handmade', and challenge the often derogatory and ageist image of those (mostly women) who choose to design and craft with yarn. I hope that by doing so I am validating the skills of so many others.

I have always loved the intricacies of crochet. I am still fascinated by how yarn and a simple hook can create the most incredible fabrics, and I adore working out stitch formations and all the technicalities that go along the way. I am a true believer in the importance of passing on skills through the generations to preserve my beloved craft, and so I am really excited to bring together some of the many tips and techniques I have learned over the years within this book. I hope you will enjoy it!

Janie
x

Jane's inspirations

Colour palette, nature, location, art and so much more inspires my crochet designs, and once you have grasped the essential and further techniques covered in this book, you may too be motivated to design your own patterns.

FIELDS OF GOLD

I love botanical drawings and have a book from Kew Gardens in London that showcases some wonderful illustrations. One page features sunflowers, hellebores and opium-poppy seedheads, and it made me think of the fields of sunflowers we walked through on a lovely French holiday some years ago.

I have always loved sunflowers, and in particular their association with heat and sunshine. Since wild poppies are commonplace in fields of sunflowers, it was logical that this design should feature these too!

The project is put together using the join-as-you-go method (see page 134) and the sunflowers feature petals made by increasing into stitches (see page 48) then forming clusters (see page 87) to decrease the stitch count.

MYSTICAL LANTERNS

This design was inspired by the "ogee" shape found in Moroccan surface pattern and architecture. The motif is curved like an onion, consisting of a concave arc and vertical ends, so that it tessellates with itself (see page 73). It took me an age to work out how to make the crochet shape tessellate, but in the end the design was very simple and uses a granny hexagon (see page 72) at the center.

Mystical Lanterns is possibly the easiest project within my design range and can be used as a great exercise for choosing a color palette, especially as I recommend that crocheters embrace the random nature of picking yarns (see page 99).

THE FRUIT GARDEN

William Morris's daughter May was a skilled artist, basing many of her designs on nature, with plants and birds some of her favourite design sources. May's passion was embroidery, and it was her skilful, innovative and beautiful stitch work that helped elevate needlework from a domestic craft to a serious art form, and her influence extended around the world.

For this design I drew inspiration from May's intricate draft drawings for her embroidery projects, as well as the embroideries themselves. Many of her designs feature flora and fauna on an embroidered trellis background, which I have emulated here.

LILY POND

During his lifetime, Claude Monet completed a series of more than 250 paintings of water lilies. Along with *Starry Night* by Vincent van Gogh, Monet's paintings are considered the most iconic examples of the Impressionist art movement.

Monet's water-lily paintings were the inspiration for this design. I wanted to create a piece that not only gave the idea of lilies on a pond, but also of the water itself, so I used lots of stitch combinations to help create the feeling of movement.

The blanket features three-dimensional crochet to emulate the flowers, and textural stitchwork (see pages 74–86), including bobbles, puffs, and fan stitches, to portray the idea of water and its reflections.

About this book

This book is organized in a logical order that takes you through the opportunities for choosing yarns, hooks and other tools, followed by practical chapters that cover the very first steps right up to embellishments and finishing touches.

HOOKS, YARNS AND OTHER ESSENTIALS
PAGES 12–23

If you have never crocheted before, the range of yarns and hooks available at craft shops may seem overwhelming. This chapter will make those choices clearer and give you an understanding of what you need to get started.

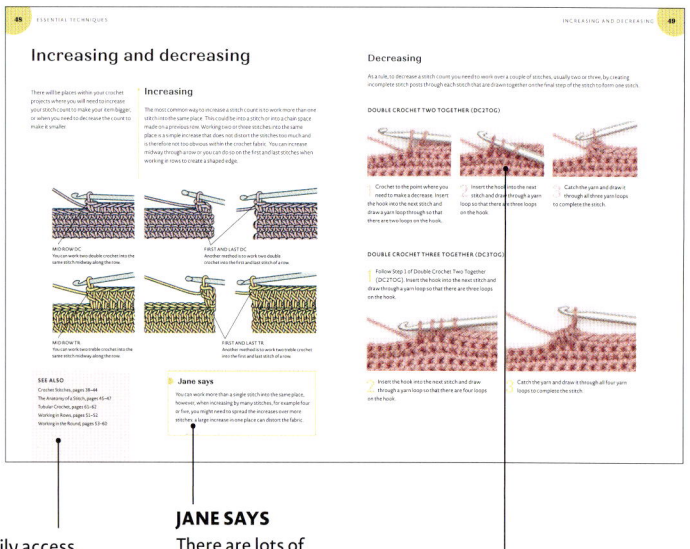

ESSENTIAL TECHNIQUES
PAGES 24–67

The first techniques chapter of the book covers all the basics, including holding the hook and yarn and reading patterns and charts, to making double, treble – and more – crochet stitches, working in rows and in the round, increasing and decreasing, and joining in new yarn.

SEE ALSO
You can easily access other sections-of-use within the book using this reference point.

JANE SAYS
There are lots of extra tips from Jane throughout the book.

WORK STEP BY STEP
Photographs and accompanying instructions show you how to work.

**SHAPES AND
STITCHES
PAGES
68–103**

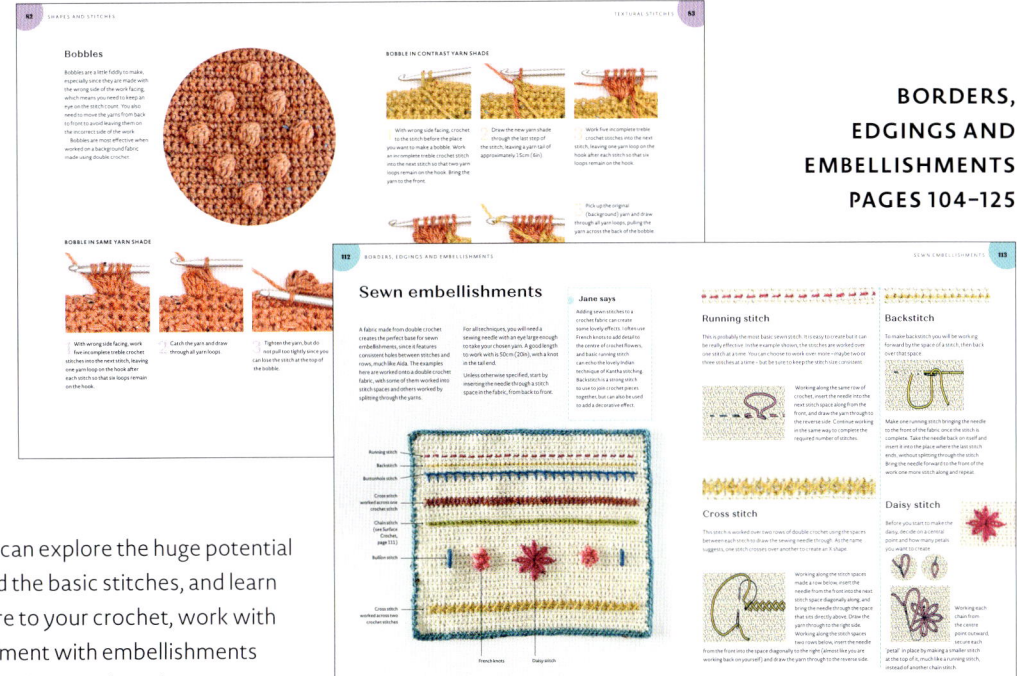

**BORDERS,
EDGINGS AND
EMBELLISHMENTS
PAGES 104–125**

This is where you can explore the huge potential of crochet beyond the basic stitches, and learn how to add texture to your crochet, work with colour and experiment with embellishments using crochet and other textile techniques.

LEFT-HANDED CROCHETERS

The photographs and illustrations in this book have been shown by a right-handed crocheter. However, that does not rule out left-handers. Here are some tips for using this book if your left hand is dominant.

EQUAL IMPORTANCE

Both hands are involved in the process of crocheting, so if you are a true beginner, it makes sense to learn to crochet right-handed, simply because it will make it much easier in terms of following written and charted instructions.

The fabric created by crocheting left-handed usually shows no difference in appearance to that made by a right-handed crocheter, although some left-handers do create a slightly more textural stitch by taking the yarn round the hook in the opposite direction when crocheting.

FLIP IT

Right-handed crocheters work in an anticlockwise direction. Left-handed crocheters work in a clockwise direction, with rows working left to right instead of right to left.

The brains of left-handed crocheters appear to manage to flip basic instructions without too much of a challenge; however, there are some areas where left-handed crocheters might find their work looks different to that of right-handers, such as when creating shapes that are not equilateral – for example, asymmetrical triangle shawls or more freeform shapes –

which will result as a mirror-image to that of a right-hander.

FOLLOWING A CHART

Charts are most commonly drawn for right-handed crocheters, so they assume that you are going to follow them in an anticlockwise direction. Left-handers can use a mobile phone to photograph the chart, and most modern mobile phones will then allow you to flip it to a mirror-image. You can then send this to your printer if you prefer to work from a paper pattern.

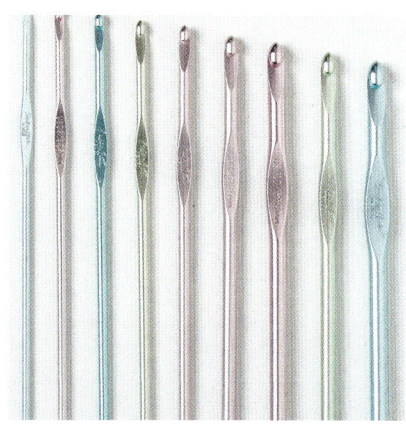

Hooks, yarns and other crochet essentials

STARTING WITH HOOKS AND YARN, THE BASICS YOU NEED
TO BEGIN CROCHETING ARE EASILY AVAILABLE, PORTABLE
AND RELATIVELY INEXPENSIVE. IN THIS CHAPTER
WE'LL CONSIDER WHAT TO THINK ABOUT WHEN
STOCKING YOUR CROCHET KIT.

All about hooks

Choosing the right hook is a little like buying a new pair of shoes: you need to find the right fit. The best way to do that is to 'try them on', or rather to test a few before deciding on which one is right for you.

Types of hook

Crochet hooks are most commonly manufactured in metal or plastic, although you can also find them made from wood or bone, especially if sourcing vintage hooks.

Many modern crochet hooks have a slim handle made from plastic or latex. These hooks with handles are referred to as ergonomic because they cut down on the stress placed on your hand when you grip them, and on the amount of movement incurred by your wrist.

Choosing a hook

It is important that your chosen hook feels comfortable in your hand as you crochet. However, trying them out in stores is extremely difficult if they are contained in packaging, and impossible if buying online. So, for a while you may need to buy and try. As your skill set and experience grow you might also find that your grip, and therefore your choice of hook, can change.

Your preferred hook hold (see page 26) will have an influence on your choice. Pencil holders are often more comfortable using a hook with a rounded handle or shaft, whereas knife holders may prefer a hook with a flat handle to place their thumb on.

SEE ALSO

Holding the Hook and Yarn, pages 26–27
Yarn Basics, pages 16–17

Anatomy of a hook

There are many crochet hooks on the market, but the basic anatomy of them remains the same. The hook end may be pointed or a little more rounded, with a rounded end more suited to softer yarns, such as wool. What you want is for the yarn to glide over the hook, not stick or get caught in the crook.

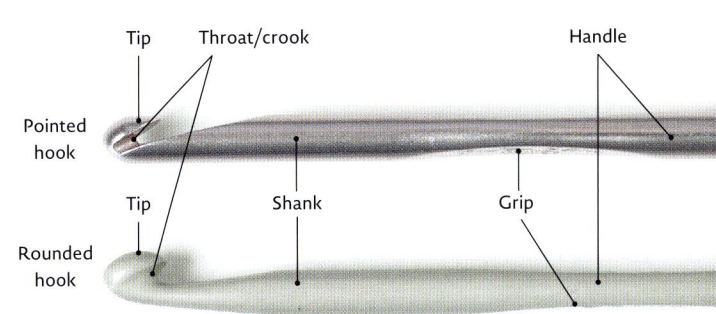

Pointed hook — Tip, Throat/crook, Handle

Rounded hook — Tip, Shank, Grip

HOOK SIZING – UK AND US

The size of hook you use should relate to a compatible yarn weight. The thicker the yarn, the larger the hook needs to be.

Detailed here are the most commonly used hook sizes.

Manufacturers use metric sizing as well as numbers and/or letters, so always check the packaging when buying a new hook when searching for a size to suit a particular pattern.

If your pattern calls for letter and number sizing that you don't recognize, look for the millimetre size closest to the one specified, to ensure the most accurate comparison.

UK	US
2.25mm	B-1
2.75mm	C-2
3.25mm	D-3
3.5mm	E-4
3.75mm	F-5
4.25mm	G
5mm	H-8
5.5mm	I-9
6mm	J-10
6.5mm	K-10½
8mm	L-11
9mm	M/N-13
10mm	N/P-15

Yarn basics

Crochet patterns will have been designed with a particular yarn in mind; however, the yarn you choose for any project is down to personal choice (see pages 20–21 for advice on adapting yarn choice). For example, you might be swayed by your wish to choose ethically, or with regard to your budget.

On these pages you will find a summary of the various types of yarn and their qualities, to help you make those all-important decisions.

SEE ALSO

Yarn Troubleshooting, pages 20–21

Animal-origin

Many yarns are made from the spun hair of animals. The most common is the wool of sheep (**7**), which is shorn from the animal. Sheep need to be shorn to keep them cool and healthy, and shearing doesn't harm the animal.

Natural animal yarns are often a little more expensive than manmade fibres, and the wool from certain breeds of sheep, such as Merino (**3**) and Shetland, is considered of a higher quality than that from other breeds.

Mohair is a fluffy yarn that comes from the coats of a breed of goat, as does cashmere and pashmina. You can also source alpaca (**6**), angora, possum and camel yarns.

Silk (**2**) is made from the threadlike lining of caterpillar cocoons. In order to not damage the thread, the cocoons are boiled with the silkworms still inside, so silk is not a vegan yarn. Yarns spun with silk have a sheen and tend to be soft.

Plant-origin

The most common yarn of plant origin is cotton (**5** and **8**), which is created from the fluffy seed coat the plant produces. Cotton takes a large amount of water to produce and is grown in countries where poverty and child labour can play a part in its production.

Linen is derived from the cellulose lining of the stalks of the flax plant. The plant itself does not require a huge amount of water or care to produce, and can crop in abundance. When crocheting, linen yarn can be a little harsh on the hands and has little give.

Semisynthetic

Bamboo yarns (**1**) are rising in popularity. The creation of the yarn involves quite a lot of processing and chemicals; however, bamboo grows very quickly and is said to absorb pollutants from the air, and so is considered a relatively good eco yarn choice.

Like linen and bamboo, viscose is made from the cellulose or wood pulp derived from fast-growing plants such as eucalyptus, beech and pine, as well as ethically harvested 'wood' from plants like bamboo, soy and sugar cane. The process of creating viscose, rayon and lyocell (also known as Tecel™) uses synthetic substances and chemicals. Cupro is made from cotton waste by regenerating cellulose.

Synthetic

Acrylic (❾) and polyester are true synthetics of petrochemical origin, and therefore can be related to plastic. Acrylic is made from a polymer called acrylonitrile, and is considered of a higher quality than polyester.

Textured and colour-change

Yarns are usually smooth, but they can have added texture in the form of slubs or bouclés. You can also buy variegated colour yarns (❹ and ❻) and those that subtly change shade as you work through the ball.

Yarn weights

Yarns traditionally sit in weight categories. Yarn weights are pretty much universal, although handspun yarns and some speciality fibres might not sit within a specific grouping.

'S' twist   'Z' twist

Yarns are made from a number of strands of thread that are twisted together to create the weight. Yarns can be spun in an 'S' or 'Z' twist. The twist can affect the softness of the yarn, and some looser-spun yarns can unravel slightly as you crochet.

The yarn weight groups have names, some of which are different depending on where in the world you are. Use the chart (below) for guidance.

1 3-ply
2 4-ply
3 DK
4 Aran
5 Chunky
6 Super chunky

UK YARN WEIGHT	US YARN WEIGHT	COMMON NAMES
2-ply (0)	Lace	Light fingering, fine, cobweb
3-ply (1)	Super fine	Sock, fingering
4-ply (2)	Fine	Sport, baby
DK (3)	Light	8-ply, jumper, light worsted
Aran (4)	Medium	Worsted, afghan
Chunky (5)	Bulky	Heavy worsted, craft, rug
Super chunky (6)	Super bulky	Bulky
–	Jumbo (7)	Roving

Thread count

It is currently fashionable to use yarns created for the handknit market to crochet with, but in the past crochet yarns used a thread count reference to differentiate the weights. If the yarn is categorized by thread count, use the chart (below) for guidance on what hook to use with it.

THREAD COUNT	HOOK SIZE (UK)
No. 5	3.5mm
No. 10	4.25mm
No. 15	4.25mm
No. 20	6mm
No. 30	6mm
No. 40	6mm
No. 50	6mm
No. 60	9mm
No. 80	9mm
No. 100	9mm

Dye lots

Yarn is created in batches, and although manufacturers use consistent methods, there can still be slight differences in shade of yarn between each batch. This is referred to as the dye lot. Stores usually check that the yarns they sell are from the same dye lot, but it's worth checking yourself on the ball band (right), and in particular if you're buying online. Differences in dye lots may seem small but can be surprisingly visible when crocheted into a fabric.

READING A BALL BAND

A ball band is a piece of paper or card attached to the yarn. If you have sourced a skein of yarn, rather than a ball, it should have a tag attached that contains some essential information.

Washing instructions

Hook/knitting needle size

Tension

Yarn fibre composition — 40% Wool 30% Acrylic 30% Polyester (all recycled)

Length of yarn — Approx 350 meters / 383 yards

Yarn weight — DK Weight

Country of origin

Colour reference

Barcode

Dye lot

Stylecraft
ReCreate
100% Recycled Yarn

100g in accordance with BS 984:1990
Made for Stylecraft under licence in Turkey
Spa Mill, New Street, Slaithwaite, HD7 5BB
www.stylecraft-yarns.co.uk
a Spectrum Yarns brand

Shade: 3375 Teal

Dye: SB27430

Yarn troubleshooting

Some common troubleshooting necessities for yarn use include swapping out a specified pattern yarn for an alternative, converting metric to imperial – or vice versa – in yarn length or weight, and what to do with knots in your yarn.

Choosing a good alternative yarn for a project

Most patterns recommend you use a specific yarn. Since the project will have been tested using that yarn, optimal results will be achieved if you use it too. However, it is not essential that you use exactly what is suggested.

Refer to the yarn weight and hook size tables on pages 18–19 to ascertain some suitable alternatives, and always look at the suggested tension on the yarn in comparison to that you want to use. If you are unsure what weight your chosen yarn is, it is essential that you make a tension sample (see pages 28–29).

Most yarns on the market fall into set categories according to their weight. Yarns sit within the categories to make it easier to ensure that things come up to the right size. This is especially handy when substituting yarn, since, in theory, a yarn weight should achieve more or less the same tension regardless of brand or yarn content. The ball band on the yarn may give you the suggested tension as well as a needle or hook size that this tension is to be achieved on.

Keep it all

Due to the nature of crochet, there is no guarantee that all crocheters will achieve the same amount of leftover yarns at the end of a project. Even the very slightest difference in motif size and tension can make a big difference to the amount of yarn used, partly because of the number of times the yarn is wrapped around the hook to make stitches.

It is a good idea to keep hold of all your yarn until the end of the project. Even the pieces you might undo, and any pieces that look frayed. Don't be tempted to use any of the yarn for another project until you have completed the current project, and make sure you keep everything in a safe place.

Metric and imperial

When substituting yarn it is important that you find one that achieves the correct tension and has enough metres of yarn on the ball. Don't assume that every ball of yarn has the same length.

Patterns written in UK terms are most likely to include measurements in centimetres. Yarn is measured in metres.

In US terms patterns include references to inches and yarn is measured in yards.

LENGTH
There are **10cm to 4in**.

1 metre is longer than a yard, at approximately $1\frac{1}{12}$ of a yard in length. **1 metre = 1.09yd.**

WEIGHT

Most yarns are sold by weight. In the UK this is measured in grams (g), with the imperial equivalent being ounces (oz).

The two most common ball or skein weights are 100g, which is $3\frac{1}{2}$oz in imperial, and 50g, which is equivalent to $1\frac{3}{4}$oz. **100g = $3\frac{1}{2}$oz. 50g = $1\frac{3}{4}$oz.**

YARN STASH

Your collection of leftover yarns, or those that you have yet to use, is referred to as a yarn stash.

Crafters have stashes of varying sizes, especially as it is worth keeping hold of yarns in case you can use them in the future. It is a good idea to organize your stash in some way, so that you have an idea of what you have. Using up yarns from your stash is called stash busting.

Because of the risk that moths and grubs can pose, it is a good idea to store your yarn in airtight containers. Some people keep their stashes in different boxes according to yarn weight, and some are so organized that they keep a list of what they have in their stash.

Various websites, such as Ravelry, provide an online area for you to list your yarns for easy reference.

What to do if there is a knot in the yarn

Unfortunately, due to the manufacturing process, you may find knots in the yarn as you are working through it. It can be frustrating to come across a knot when you are in the throes of a project, so it is a good idea to check through for knots before you start: some crocheters like to rewind the ball before they start stitching.

You do not want a knot to become trapped in your stitches midway through a row of crochet, since it could come undone, so, if you spot a knot, unravel the work to a point where you can create a safe change over, such as a side edge or seam. Cut the knot away and join in the new yarn end.

What else is in the kit?

On top of your hook and yarn, there is not a lot else you need in your crochet kit. Start with scissors and dressmaking pins, then build your supplies as you realize what you need, or perhaps just what would be nice to have.

❶ SCISSORS
Use small, sharp scissors to clip yarn ends.

❷ STRAIGHT PINS
You'll need these when you measure tension and block your completed crochet projects.

❸ YARN CUTTER
Yarn cutters are a great alternative to a pair of scissors, especially when travelling. The sharp blade is hidden within a casing so you won't cut your fingers when breaking yarn.

❹ RULER AND TAPE MEASURE
Use a ruler when measuring tension swatches, and a tape measure for your larger pieces.

❺ STITCH MARKERS
Stitch markers are a life saver for crocheters. Use them to mark repeats and increases, as well as stitch and chain numbers. Some markers look like little pins, while others are like small split rings. You can also use a larger style that has a clip that lets you add a paper note, which is particularly handy when keeping track of row and stitch counts.

❻ BEADS

Crochet stitches alone give a wealth of opportunities to include texture and interest in the making of the fabric, but you can also add extra decoration using beads or sequins.

❼ TAPESTRY NEEDLE

These needles have a blunter end than dressmaking needles and are used to add sewn embellishments – embroidery stitches and beads, for example – to your crochet fabric.

❽ NOTE-TAKING SUPPLIES

A good way of ensuring you are working in the correct way is to keep notes. Using a pencil to mark a pattern or make notes is safer than using a pen because you can erase marks if need be. Yarn cards can help you keep track of yarn shade names and numbers too.

ROW COUNTER

You can keep track of your crochet rows by making notes on paper, but row counters can make the process much easier. Many are barrel shaped with a counter that is turned to add up after each row.

BOBBINS

You can make your own butterfly bobbin (see page 100) or source plastic versions that you then wind your yarn around.

HOOK GAUGE

Modern hooks tend to have their size marked on them (usually on the handle), but older hooks won't necessarily do so. You can use a hook gauge to check the size – be careful if the hook has a sloped shaft, and measure close to the hook end.

ROLLS AND CASES

Having a crochet hook roll means you can store all your hooks and keep them clean. Rolls are especially good as they create compact storage, but larger pencil cases can also work.

BAGS AND POUCHES

When not working on your crochet, keep projects in bags with a secure fastener to ensure you don't lose anything between use.

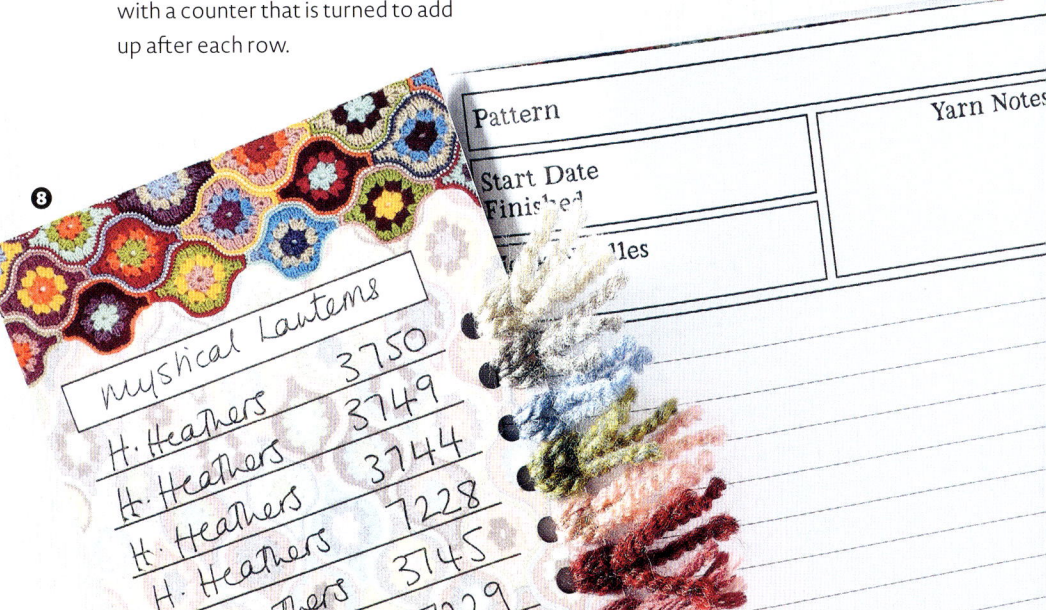

Essential techniques

EVERY CHAIN AND EVERY STITCH CONTRIBUTE TO THE FINAL LOOK OF A PROJECT. IN THIS CHAPTER WE LOOK AT THE ESSENTIAL TECHNIQUES OF CROCHET AND WAYS TO ELEVATE THEM.

Holding the hook and yarn

Above all else, when it comes to holding your hook and yarn, it is important to be comfortable.

The more you practise crochet, the more likely you are to find a way of holding the hook that suits you, so don't let anyone tell you there is a right or wrong way; you will find what works best for you!

That said, there are two holds that are generally recommended when you first learn to crochet, referred to as pencil and knife holds. If you find a different way that suits you and doesn't aggravate your wrist or put undue pressure on your fingers, then go with that.

The way you hold the hook is the same regardless of which hand is your dominant one. The only difference is that when crocheting right-handed the hook is held in the right hand and the yarn in the left hand, and vice versa for crocheting left-handed.

Pencil hold

Imagine you are holding a pen or a pencil in the way that you were taught at school, and adapt this slightly for holding the crochet hook. If the hook has a flat part on the handle or shaft, then this is where your thumb should sit, with the hook itself pointing towards you. The shaft should sit in the crook of your hand between your thumb and index finger, with your index finger applying slight pressure to the side of the hook. Your middle finger provides support for the hook from underneath, and your remaining fingers sit below.

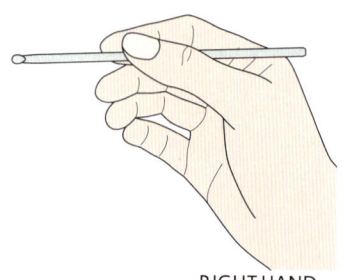

RIGHT HAND

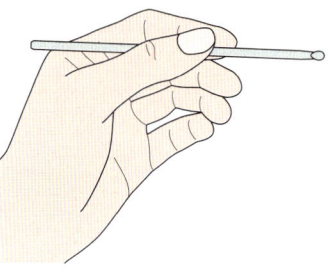

LEFT HAND

Knife hold

Sometimes referred to as top hold, imagine you are holding a knife and are about to cut through some food on your plate. If the hook has a flat part on the handle or shaft, this is where your thumb should sit, with the hook itself pointing towards you. The shaft should sit inside the grip of your hand, but not too tightly since your index finger should be able to move around to guide your stitches off the hook. Your middle finger and ring finger act as support, and your little finger is likely to curl itself around the hook.

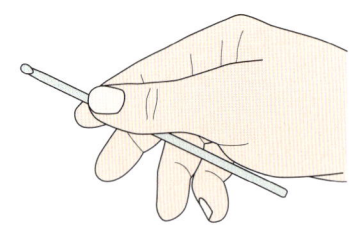

RIGHT HAND

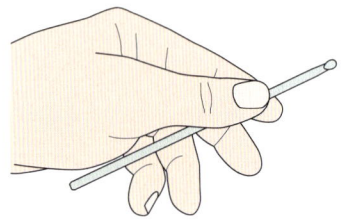

LEFT HAND

SEE ALSO

Starting with a Slipknot, page 34

Movement

Whichever way you choose to hold the hook, it is important that you do not grip it too tightly, since the shaft needs to be able to roll around in your hand so that the hook itself can change position. Have a play around with how you feel comfortable, and don't be afraid to change the way you hold the hook as you become more competent.

Holding the yarn

Both hands are very much involved in the act of crocheting, and one of the most difficult actions to learn as a beginner is the movement of the non-dominant hand.

Whether you use the pencil or knife hold, you need to provide tension on the yarn with the thumb, index and middle finger of the opposite hand. Once you have placed a slipknot on the hook, the yarn end that is still attached to the ball goes over the index finger then through the grip of your hand so that your ring finger and little finger can provide tension. Your thumb and middle finger gently grip the slipknot below the hook and are repositioned every few stitches.

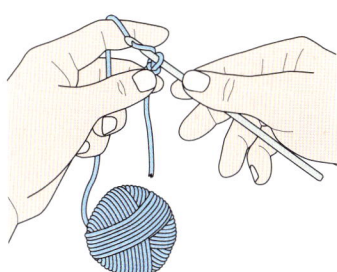

If you hold the hook in your right hand, hold the yarn in your left hand.

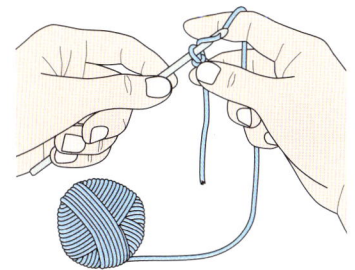

If you hold the hook in your left hand, hold the yarn in your right hand, but still place the ball on your left side to make it easier to pull and tension the yarn.

Avoiding aches, pains and physical stresses

Repetitive actions and prolonged activity can put stress on parts of the body. It is important that you don't cause yourself an injury by putting too much pressure on your hands or by making unnatural movements. Your wrist is particularly susceptible to too much twisting and turning, while watching the hook and yarn as you create stitches can lead to poor, slightly hunched posture.

Crocheting for hours on end is not a great idea if you want to avoid aches and pains, so make sure you take a break every so often. Release your grip on the yarn and hook and stretch out your fingers. Sit up straight and roll your head and neck from side to side, and pull your shoulders back to expand your chest.

If you wear glasses, make sure you use the correct pair and that you can clearly see what you are doing. Crocheting in a well-lit position is also a good idea.

Above all else, if you feel any pain, it is important that you stop what you are doing rather than carrying on.

Jane says

If you holding the yarn uncomfortable, or that it creates pressure on any part of your hand or wrist, adapt the hold to suit you. When I first started to crochet I used my right hand to wrap the yarn around my hook as if I was knitting, and later taught my left hand to hold the yarn.

If you are left-handed and have never crocheted before, my recommendation is that you learn the right-handed method. If you have already learned to crochet left-handed then, of course, stick with your tried-and-tested technique.

Tension

When working through a crochet project, especially one that needs to come out to a specific size, it is important that you achieve the correct tension. The word tension is used to refer to the number of stitches and rows or rounds that is achieved over a specific measurement. Achieving the correct tension will mean that your crochet project will ultimately be the right size.

The standard recommended tension for knitting is often shown on the yarn ball band, but it is rare to find the crochet tension on there too, so you will need to refer to your crochet pattern to find out the approximate measurements you should be achieving when you work your stitches.

Jane says

Crochet projects that do not have a specified size to work to – such as a granny-square afghan using stash yarns – do not require you to work to a definite tension; however, it is always worth considering tension as you work through a project to ensure that your pieces all end up a similar size, and that your yarn use is consistent throughout.

SEE ALSO

Counting Rows, page 51

Counting Rounds, page 60

Counting Stitches, page 47

Patterns and Charts, pages 30–33

The Anatomy of a Stitch, pages 45–47

Measuring tension

Some patterns will include tension measurements under the yarn and equipment guide, some will only give you a finished project measurement, while some will give you measurements within the instructions so that you check you are working to tension as you progress through the project. If you are making repeated motifs that are going to be joined together later, your pattern might give you the measurements of a single motif.

Regardless of the project you are working on, it is a good idea to start by creating a tension swatch. Putting time in to do this at the start of a project (even though you will be eager to get going on the main pattern) could save you lots of time and heartache later!

Make a swatch that is a little bigger than the area the tension is to be measured over. So, if your pattern states that the tension is measured over 10cm (4in), make a swatch that is half this size again, 15cm (6in) square. Edge stitches love to curl, so working a larger swatch means that you can measure a true tension towards the centre of the swatch.

You should also make your test piece using the same yarn and hook as you intend to use for the project, since these factors will affect tension.

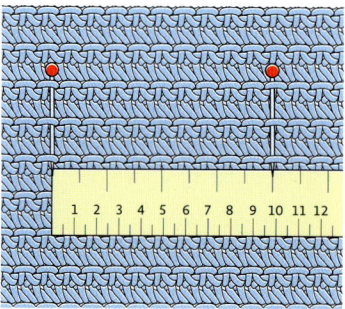 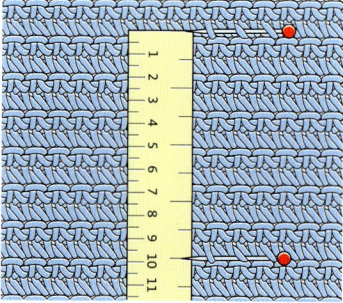

1 Use a ruler to position pins in the swatch to denote the area of the tension measurement – in this case that is 10cm (4in) square. Count the number of stitches between the pins, including half stitches.

2 Position the ruler vertically, place pins as before, and count the rows or rounds, including any partial rows.

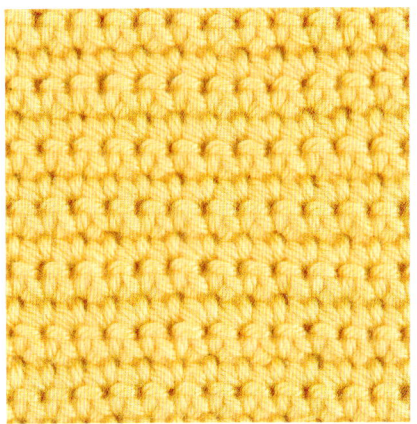

TENSION IS TOO TIGHT

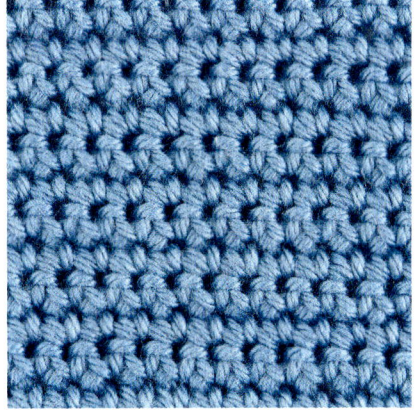

TENSION IS GOOD

TENSION IS TOO LOOSE

How to change your tension

If you achieve the correct number of stitches and rows or rounds, you can go ahead with your project, pretty confident that it will come out the right size.

If you achieve too many stitches to the measurement then you are working to a tight tension, and conversely, if you achieve too few stitches you are working too loosely.

TOO TIGHT

- Rather than trying to change your crochet method (by consciously crocheting more loosely) simply change to a larger hook size. If you are still too tight, try another size larger.
- If your project uses multiple hook sizes, make a note of how many sizes you have had to change by to ensure you make the swap throughout the project.

TOO LOOSE

- Rather than trying to change your crochet method (by consciously crocheting more tightly), change to a smaller hook size. If you are still too loose, try another size smaller.
- If your project uses multiple hook sizes, make a note of how many sizes you have had to change by to ensure you make the swap throughout the project.

RIGHT STITCH COUNT, INCORRECT ROW COUNT, AND VICE VERSA

You might find that you achieve the correct stitch count but incorrect row count, or the opposite, where you have the rows right but the stitch count wrong. If you have tried all the tips for achieving the correct tension but still have a problem, you need to decide which tension is more important and choose between that of the stitches or of the rows.

Jane says

Even if you are a crochet pro it is worth checking your tension when embarking on a new project, since different yarns and stitches can influence your work, as can your mood or the situation in which you are crocheting.

MEASURING TECHNIQUE

Whether you are measuring tension, or measuring as you work a project, always measure on a flat surface and, since crochet loves to curl up, make sure you also smooth out the edges of the work. It can be helpful to pin your work in place, but be careful not to stretch it.

When measuring small-enough pieces of work, use a ruler rather than a tape measure, since these can stretch over time. Aim to use the same ruler throughout and always include even the smallest of measurements, rather than rounding size up or down. For inches this means including each eighth of an inch.

Patterns and charts

Traditional crochet patterns – such as those from the 1950s – assume that the crocheter is adept at understanding very basic instructions. Old crochet patterns can almost look like they are written in a secret code, with only a list of very brief abbreviations to go by. Thankfully, these days patterns are much more informative.

The best patterns are those that provide written instructions alongside charts or graphics, and even step-by-step images.

Yarn and equipment details   Instructions for less common stitches

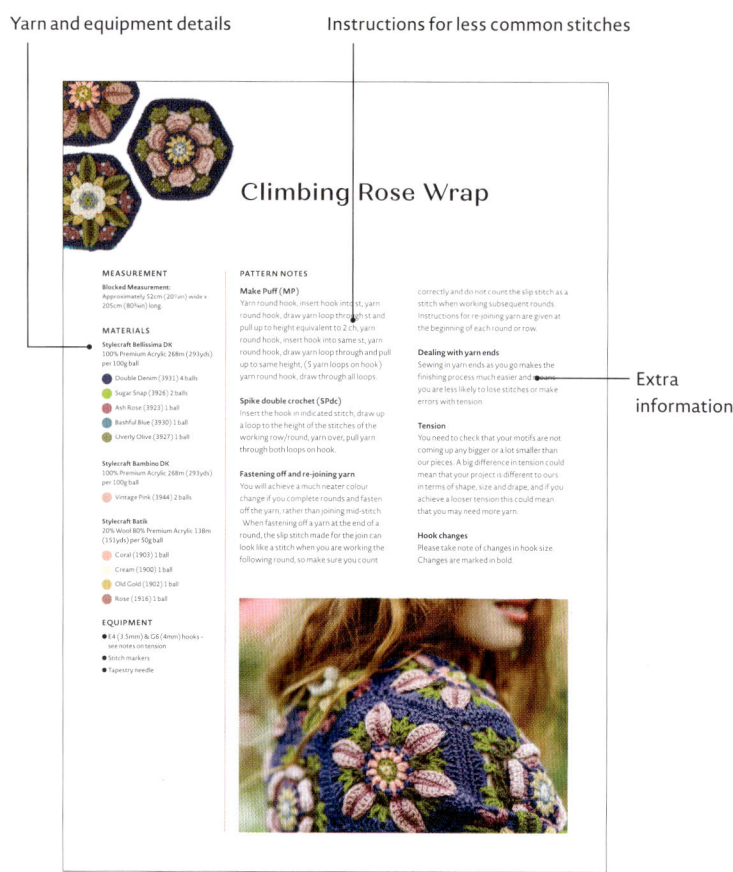

Extra information

SEE ALSO

Common Chart Symbols, page 138

Common Pattern Abbreviations, page 138

Tension, pages 28–29

The Anatomy of a Stitch, pages 45–47

Reading a pattern

To read and understand a written pattern you need to have a knowledge of the abbreviations for stitches (see page 138). Most patterns will assume you know basic abbreviations but may include an explanation for more complex or unusual stitches in an abbreviated form.

Most crochet patterns are written in a common formulaic way. They will start by asking you to make a number of chains (chain stitches), which are then used to form the basis of your crochet. They will then tell you how many stitches and rows to work.

For example:

Row 1: ch 3, 2 dc in first dc, dc in each rem dc across to last dc, 2 dc in last dc, turn.

TERMINOLOGY

There is a difference in crochet terminology between the UK and the US. If the names of the stitches were completely different it would be easy to recognize a UK or US pattern, but they use many of the same terms, just for different stitches.

This chart translates UK and US stitch names and their abbreviations.

UK		US	
double crochet	dc	single crochet	sc
half treble crochet	htc	half double crochet	hdc
treble crochet	tr	double crochet	dc
double treble crochet	dtr	treble crochet	tr
triple treble crochet	trtr	double treble crochet	dtr

Multiples and repeats

To keep written instructions as brief as possible you will often be asked to work multiple repeats. These are usually written in a standard way using asterisks and semicolons as well as square and rounded brackets.

ASTERISKS AND SEMICOLONS

Asterisks * and semicolons ; are used when the pattern involves a relatively long repeat, and in all cases you are being asked to complete a pattern repeat that starts at the asterisk and ends at the semicolon. You may be asked to repeat a specific number of times, or to the end of the row or round.

For example:
Row 2: ch 3, *2 dc in first dc, dc in each rem dc across to last st; repeat from * five times.
Row 3: ch 3, *2 dc in first dc, dc in each rem dc across to last st; repeat from * to end.

ROUNDED BRACKETS

When working a short repeat into a single stitch, or a small group of stitches, rounded brackets ( ) may be used, in which case you are being asked to repeat the instructions detailed between the rounded brackets.

For example:
(1 dc, 1 htr, 1 tr) into next st or (1 dc, 1 htr, 1 tr) over next 3 sts.

SQUARE BRACKETS

When working a shorter repeat you may find the pattern uses square brackets [ ]. This means you are being asked to repeat the instructions detailed between the square brackets.

For example:
[1 dc into next st, 1 htr into next st] to end or
[1 dc into next st, 1 htr into next st] five times.

WORK AS SET

To keep a pattern even shorter and more concise, the instruction: 'work as set to end' or 'work as set' (for a certain number of stitches or rows) may be used.

For example:
Repeat as set by Row 1 and Row 2 to desired length.

Crochet patterns are not all the same!

Crochet patterns should follow a similar layout, with the yarn and equipment details at the beginning, along with a list of abbreviations and terminology used. This could be followed by any special instructions before the method of working is explained.

When working a garment, the back of the piece is explained first, followed by the front and sleeves, with the necklines, button bands (if applicable), and making-up instructions coming later. A pattern for an afghan would probably explain how to make your motifs first, followed by making-up instructions and those for any edgings or special features.

Compare patterns written by different designers, pattern houses or yarn companies and you should find they follow this outline. However, you are also likely to discover that each of them has a slightly different way of laying the pattern out, or an alternative way of describing their abbreviations. Some designers write in a concise way, while others include a wordier explanation. Designers call this their house style.

Jane says

When writing patterns the aim is to make the instructions clear to the crocheter, whatever their level of expertise might be. If I can, I include charts and step-by-step images with my patterns, to make them as foolproof as possible.

SIZE OF PROJECT

It is not always imperative that you achieve the exact finished measurements when making a project. For example, when making a mandala or an afghan a slight difference in size is not a problem. However, to make a garment that will fit to the expected size, you need to be sure you work to the correct tension and therefore that you select the right size to make.

When making a garment for yourself or a friend or relative, look at the finished measurements rather than the standard clothing size or chest measurements. If possible, find an existing garment that fits well and is similar in style to the item you wish to make. Take a few measurements from this garment and check them against the finished measurements in the pattern. Do this before you embark on a project to potentially save time and heartache later.

Understanding charts

Crochet charts are a relatively new innovation that provide a visual reference of how your crochet should look. Chart symbols are universal and are not governed by the language your pattern is written in.

Each symbol on the chart represents a stitch or instruction, which are usually shown on an accompanying key. In most cases, the size of the symbol is relative to the size of the stitch it represents. For example, the symbol for double crochet sits at about half the height of a treble crochet symbol.

Most symbols have a vertical line that represents the post of the stitch (see The Anatomy of a Stitch, pages 45–47). Some symbols have a slash line across this vertical line to indicate how many times to wrap the yarn around the hook. For example, a symbol for a double crochet has one slash across the vertical post line and a treble crochet symbol has two.

The symbol for a chain is an oval that can be drawn at any angle and any size on a chart. The size of the oval could change to fit the chart to its layout, so larger chain symbols on the chart do not mean you need to achieve a looser tension.

Most charts are created in black type. Some will show alternate rows or rounds in grey to help you see how many to work. Some charts are shown in colour.

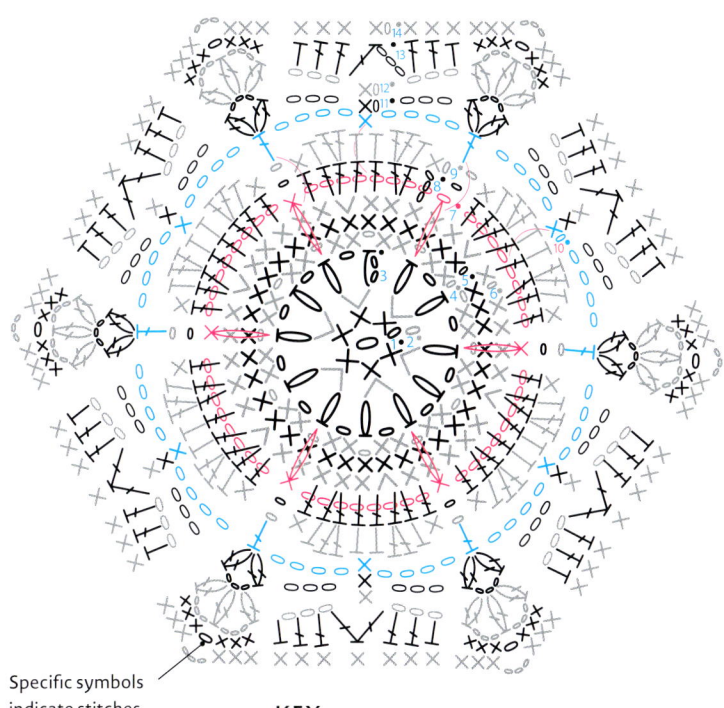

Specific symbols indicate stitches or instructions.

Key for symbols

KEY

○ chain stitch

• slip stitch

✕ double crochet (dc)

↑ spike double crochet

∨ 2dc worked in 1 stitch

T half treble crochet (htr)

Ŧ treble crochet (tr)

Ŧ double treble crochet (dtr)

U puff stitch (MP)

↶ indicates stitch placement

MAKING A LEFT-HANDED CHART

Charts are most commonly drawn for right-handed crocheters and assume that you will follow them in an anticlockwise direction. You can flip a right-handed chart using the camera on your mobile phone, and send the mirror-image to a printer if you prefer to work from a paper pattern.

Jane says

When working from a written pattern that doesn't have a chart, you might find it useful to draw out your own charts or shorthand so that you have a quick reference for what you need to do. For example:

Round 1: 1 ch (does not count as a st), *1 dc into each next 3 sts, 1 htr into each next 2 sts, 1 tr into each next 2 sts, 1 dtr into each next 3 sts, 1 tr into each next 2 sts, 1 htr into each next 2 sts; repeat from * to end.

You could note this down as follows:

1 ch, *1 dc x 3, 1 htr x 2, 1 tr x 2, 1 dtr x 3, 1 tr x 2, 1 htr x 2

Or draw as chart symbols as follows:

0 * + + + T T T Ŧ Ŧ Ŧ Ŧ Ŧ Ŧ Ŧ T T ;

Making chains

Chains are the starting point for crocheting in rows or in the round. They can be referred to simply as chains, as foundation chains, or as turning chains, depending on where they are used.

The abbreviation for a chain is ch, with multiples written as chs.

Making a foundation chain is equivalent to creating the cast on when knitting. A row of foundation chains is worked into to create the first (foundation) row of crochet. When working in the round, a sequence of chains is connected with a slip stitch.

Starting with a slipknot

Before making a sequence of chains you need to create a slipknot so that you have a yarn loop on the hook.

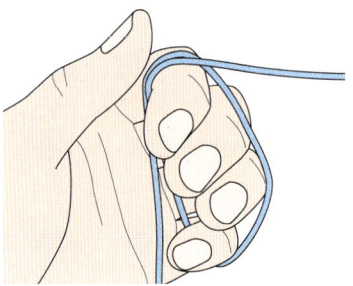

1 Leaving a tail of yarn at least 10cm (4in) long, wrap the yarn across your fingers to create a loop of yarn around your hand, making sure that the yarn is crossed over.

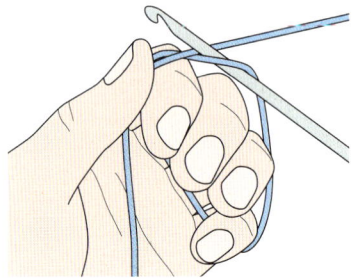

2 With the hook facing downwards, insert it into the yarn loop around your hand. Catch the yarn that leads to the ball (not the tail end) onto the hook and draw it through the loop around your hand.

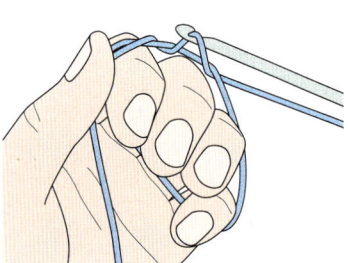

3 Rotate the hook to face upward so you are less likely to drop the yarn loop off the hook.

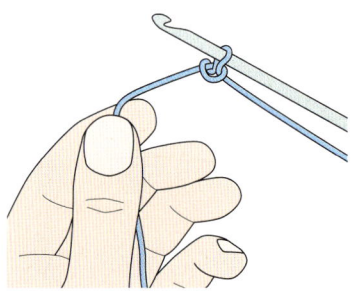

4 Gently pull on the tail end of yarn to tighten the slipknot. The slipknot will move along the yarn towards the hook. Try not to overtighten the slipknot since this will make it more difficult to create your first chain.

Making the chain

Once you have a slipknot on the hook you can start to create a chain. A chain is made by passing one yarn loop through another using your crochet hook.

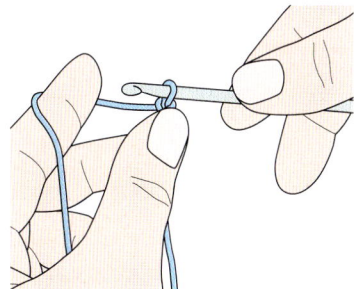

1 Hold the slipknot gently between your middle finger and thumb to add tension to the tail end of yarn. Hold the yarn that leads towards the ball over your fingers in whichever way feels comfortable.

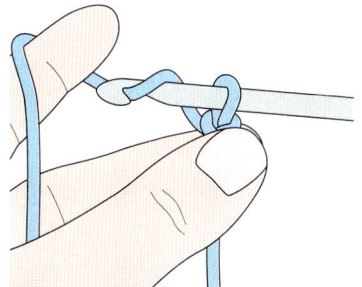

2 With the hook facing away from you, gently push it against the yarn and rotate it until the hook is facing downwards and catching the yarn in its crook.

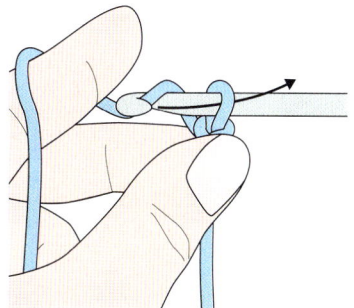

3 Gently draw the yarn through the yarn loop created by the slipknot, rotating the hook back to an upward-facing position as you do so.

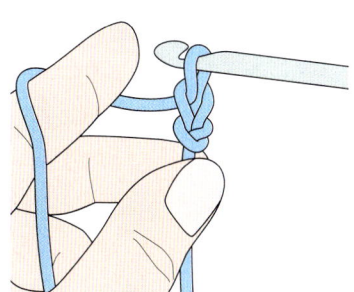

4 Chains made where the hook is finer will be tighter, so slide the yarn loop onto the shaft of the hook so that it reaches the correct tension. This counts as one chain (1 ch).

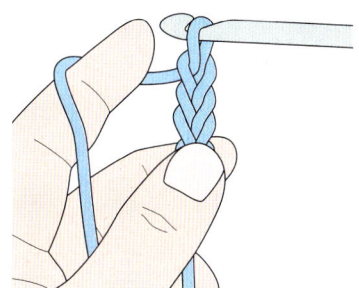

5 To create more chains, repeat the process of using the hook to catch the yarn through the yarn loops on the hook. You will need to reposition your fingers every few chains to create an even tension.

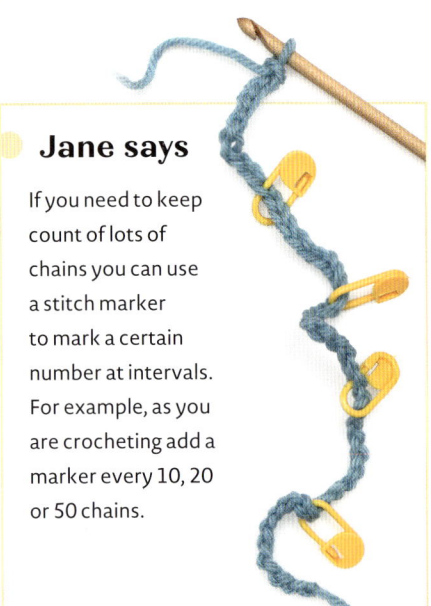

Jane says

If you need to keep count of lots of chains you can use a stitch marker to mark a certain number at intervals. For example, as you are crocheting add a marker every 10, 20 or 50 chains.

Counting chains

When it comes to counting how many chains you have made, the best advice is to count them as you make them. This is relatively easy to do when you aren't making a large number; however, it can get harder the more you make, plus, long chains can become twisted and uneven, which can make them more difficult to count.

It is always better to have too many chains than too few. If you think you are close to the correct number, but lose count as you make your chain, add on a few more, then undo any extra chains from the slipknot end once you have worked the next (foundation) row.

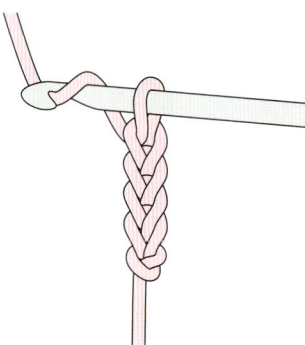

The easiest way to count the chain is from the front. From this side the chain looks like a plait.

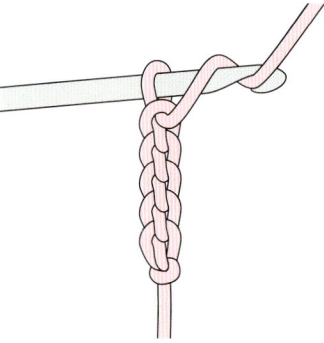

From the reverse side the chain has a vertical 'bump' of yarn.

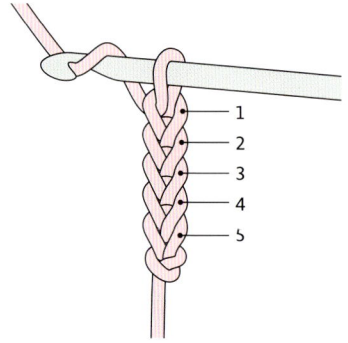

Start under the hook and count down towards the slipknot. The yarn loop on the hook does not count as a stitch.

Working into the chain to make the foundation row

When working into the chain to create a row of crochet (see pages 38–39) you can insert the hook into the chain so that you have either one or two yarn loops on the hook.

Working with two yarn loops on top of the hook and one under it will give a firmer foundation row compared to working with one loop on top of the hook and two underneath it.

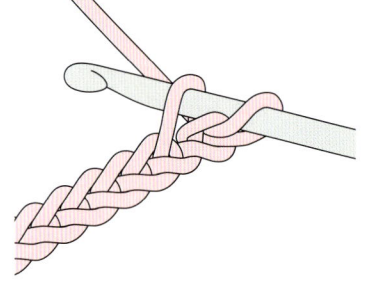

ONE LOOP ON THE HOOK

TWO LOOPS ON THE HOOK

Not enough chains?

If you get to the end of your foundation row and realize you do not have enough chains, you can make some extra using the tail end of yarn. This only works if you need to make a couple of chains rather than a large number, and have a relatively long tail end of yarn left after the slipknot. This example shows the stitches being made using double crochet.

1 Wrap the tail end of yarn around your thumb from front to back so that the yarn crosses and forms a loop on your thumb.

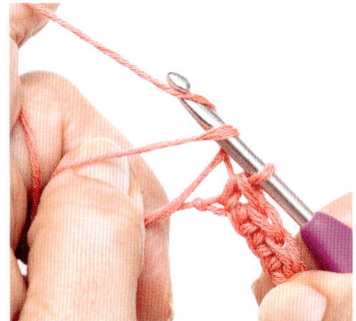

2 Keeping the loop on your thumb, while also keeping tension on the ball end of the yarn, insert the hook into the yarn loop on your thumb. Wrap the ball end of yarn around the hook.

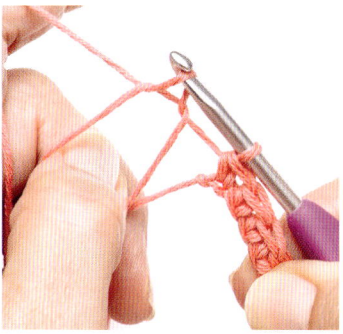

3 Draw the yarn through the loop on your thumb.

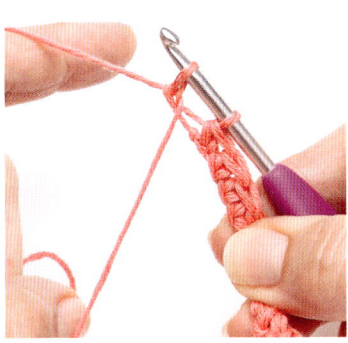

4 Remove your thumb from the yarn loop and pull the yarn ends gently to tighten – although not too tightly!

5 Wrap the yarn around the hook.

6 Draw through both yarn loops to complete the stitch.

Crochet stitches

The very first row or round of crochet stitches is different to subsequent rows or rounds, because you work into the chain; therefore, the first row is often referred to as a foundation row or foundation ring. Once you have completed your foundation row or ring you continue by working into stitches you have already made, rather than into the chain.

Rotate the hook

When making your crochet stitches it is essential that you rotate the hook to catch the yarn around the hook and draw it through chains or stitches to create more stitches. Hold the hook in a way that you can make gentle rotations. Note the position of the yarn and hook in the step-by-step images.

Double crochet (dc) into the foundation chain

1 Once you have made the required number of chains, position the part of the chain closest to the hook so that you can use your fingers to keep the tension.

2 Miss the last chain stitch you made and insert the hook into the next chain along – the second chain from the hook.

3 With the hook facing forward again, take the yarn over the hook. Rotate the hook so it faces downwards to catch the yarn in the crook.

SEE ALSO
Making Chains, pages 34–37
Turning Chains, page 44
Working in Rows, pages 51–52

4 Draw the yarn through the chain. Two yarn loops are on the hook.

5 With the hook facing forward again, take the yarn over the hook. Rotate the hook to face downwards and catch the yarn in the crook.

6 Draw the yarn through both yarn loops on the hook to complete the stitch, rotating the hook to the upwards position as you do so. One yarn loop remains on the hook.

Double crochet (dc) into the previous row

From front to back, insert the hook under the chain that sits at the top of the stitch at the base of the first chain, then follow Steps 3–6 of Double Crochet (dc) Into The Foundation Chain.

Chainless foundation row

You can create the equivalent of a foundation chain and the foundation row at the same time by making a chainless foundation row. The example here is written for double crochet, but you can adapt it for any stitch by working a longer turning chain at the beginning. For example, add one more chain for half treble crochet and another two chains for treble crochet.

1 Make two chains. Insert the hook into the second chain from the hook – the first chain made.

2 Wrap the yarn round the hook and draw it through the chain only.

3 Wrap the yarn around the hook and draw it through the next loop on the hook, which makes the equivalent of the foundation chain.

4 Wrap the yarn round the hook and draw it through both loops on the hook to make a double crochet stitch.

5 To make the next stitch, insert the hook into the yarn loop at the base of the last stitch and repeat from Step 2 until you have created the required number of stitches.

Half treble crochet (htr) into the foundation chain

When working half treble crochet the chain made at the beginning of the row or round will count as a stitch. For half treble crochet this is two chains (see Turning Chains, page 44).

1 Once you have made the required number of chain stitches, position the part of the chain closest to the hook so that you can use your fingers to keep the tension. If you are at the beginning of the row make 2 ch to count as your first stitch. Miss these 2 ch when working your next stitch.

2 To make a stitch, wrap the yarn around the hook.

3 Insert the hook into the next chain. Wrap the yarn around the hook. Rotate the hook so it faces downwards to catch the yarn in the crook.

4 Draw the yarn through the chain. Three yarn loops are on the hook. Wrap the yarn around the hook again.

5 Draw the yarn through all three loops on the hook to complete the stitch, rotating the hook to the upward position as you do so. One yarn loop remains on the hook.

Half treble (htr) crochet into the previous row

1 Make two chain stitches (this is the turning chain that counts as your first stitch). Wrap the yarn around the hook.

2 Miss the stitch at the base of the second chain. From front to back, insert the hook under the chain that sits at the top of the next stitch. Follow Steps 3–8 of Half Treble Crochet (htr) Into The Foundation Chain.

3 When working the next row you will need to work the final stitch into the second chain of the two turning chains that you made at the beginning of the last row.

Treble crochet (tr) into the foundation chain

When working treble crochet the chain made at the beginning of the row or round will count as a stitch. For treble crochet this is three chains (see Turning Chains, page 44).

1 Once you have made the required number of chains, position the part of the chain closest to the hook so that you can use your fingers to keep the tension. Wrap the yarn around the hook.

2 Miss the last three chains you made and insert the hook into the next chain along. This is the fourth chain from the hook.

3 With the hook facing forward, take the yarn over the hook.

4 Rotate the hook so it faces downwards to catch the yarn in the crook. Draw the yarn through the chain. There are three yarn loops on the hook.

5 With the hook facing forward, take the yarn over the hook.

6 Rotate the hook so it faces downwards to catch the yarn in the crook. Draw the yarn through two yarn loops on the hook. Two yarn loops are on the hook

7 Catch the yarn around the hook again and draw through the last two yarn loops on the hook to complete the stitch. One yarn loop remains on the hook.

Treble crochet (tr) into the previous row

1 Make three chains (this is the turning chain that counts as your first stitch). Wrap the yarn around the hook.

2 Miss the stitch at the base of the third chain. From front to back, insert the hook under the chain that sits at the top of the next stitch.

3 Follow Steps 3–7 of Treble Crochet (dc) Into The Foundation Chain.

4 When working the next row you will need to work the final stitch into the third chain of the three turning chains that you made at the beginning of the last row.

Turning chains

Creating rows of crochet is a little like planning to build a brick wall. Before starting a row by working repeated stitches you need to set the height of your row by creating some chains. These are referred to as turning chains and are abbreviated as either tch or tchs. A different number is worked for each particular stitch.

Depending on the height of the post of the stitch, the turning chain can count as your first stitch of the row. A well-written pattern will tell you whether the chain made at the beginning of the row counts as a stitch.

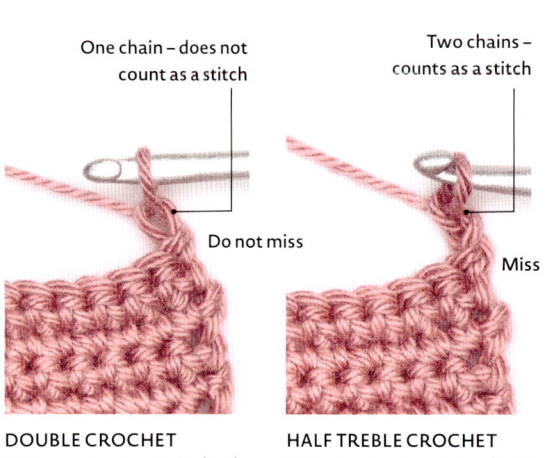

One chain – does not count as a stitch

Do not miss

DOUBLE CROCHET
Make one turning chain (1ch).

Two chains – counts as a stitch

Miss

HALF TREBLE CROCHET
Make two turning chains (2ch).

Three chains – counts as a stitch

Miss

TREBLE CROCHET
Make three turning chains (3ch).

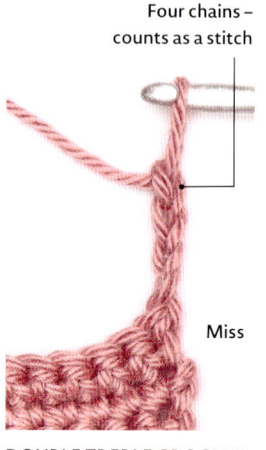

Four chains – counts as a stitch

Miss

DOUBLE TREBLE CROCHET
Make four turning chains (4ch).

When the turning chain counts as a stitch, you need to miss the stitch at the base of the chain and work into the next one when you make your second stitch of the row, unless you are told otherwise. If you have worked a turning chain at the beginning of a row, on your next row you need to work your final stitch into the final chain of the turning chain, to keep the correct stitch count.

If you find that your turning chain tends to be a little loose and you consistently create a bit of a loop at the sides of your work, try making one chain fewer than the instruction suggests. Conversely, you could make more chains if you find your turning chain is coming up a little tight.

How to fasten off when working in rows

When you get to the very end you need to fasten off in a way that ensures your work doesn't unravel.

1 When you have completed your final stitch make an extra chain. Keeping the hook within the yarn loop if possible, cut the yarn, leaving a tail end of at least 10cm (4in).

2 Gently pull the yarn end through the loop on the hook. Pull the yarn tail to tighten the last chain and create a small knot.

The anatomy of a stitch

A crochet stitch acts like a clamp, in that it encompasses part of a previous chain or stitch in the process of being made. This means that the stitch or chain made below a new stitch looks different to the new one.

Crochet stitches have a vertical post and a chain at the top. The post of the stitch will differ in height depending on which stitch you have made. The more times the yarn is wrapped around the hook before you start to make the stitch, the taller the stitch post will be. The chain at the top of a stitch is often only visible on the final row since it will have been encompassed within the stitches when making previous rows.

Double crochet

The vertical post of this stitch looks like a 'v.' A chain sits horizontally at the top of the post.

FRONT   BACK

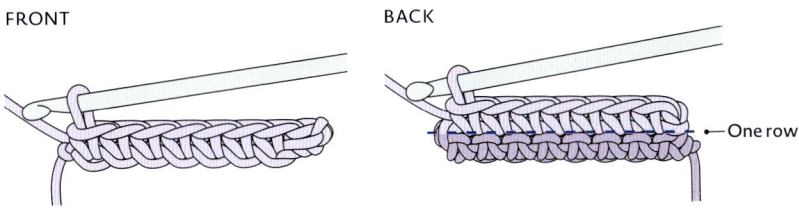

←One row

Half treble crochet

The vertical post of this stitch looks like a 'v' with another yarn sitting at a slight angle above it. A chain sits horizontally at the top of the post.

FRONT   BACK

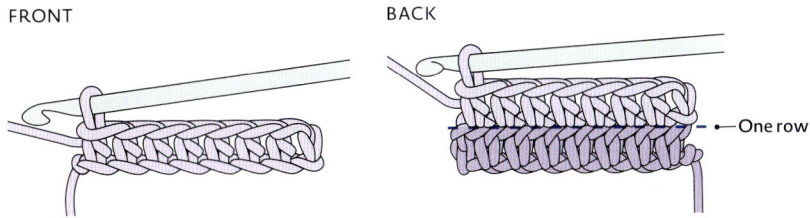

←One row

Treble crochet

The vertical post of this stitch looks like it has a 'v' at the very base with another yarn sitting at a slight angle approximately halfway up the post. A chain sits horizontally at the top of the post.

FRONT   BACK

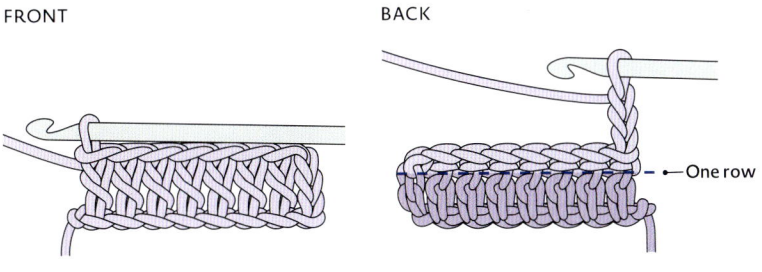

←One row

SEE ALSO

Crochet Stitches, pages 38–44
Working in Rows, pages 51–52

Double treble crochet

The vertical post of this stitch looks like it has a 'v' at the very base with two more yarns sitting at a slight angle along the post. A chain sits horizontally at the top of the post.

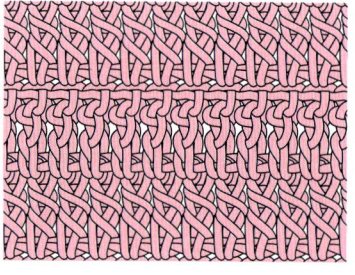

FRONT

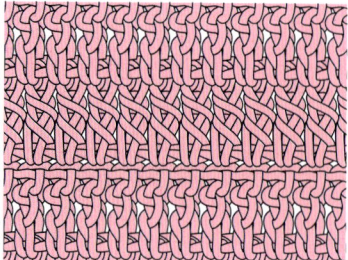

BACK

Alignment

Unlike with knitting, where the stitches are formed side by side and line up directly above each other on subsequent rows, crochet stitches sit on top of one another in an 'offset' way, like a brick wall.

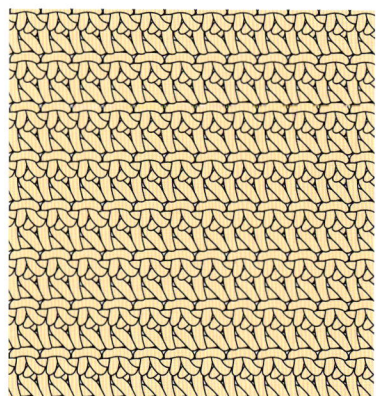

DOUBLE CROCHET

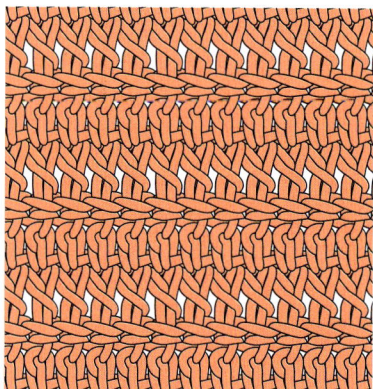

TREBLE CROCHET

DOUBLE TREBLE CROCHET

This is very apparent when working in rows, and not so obvious when working in the round, and explains why you need to add and miss stitches at the end of rows.

Using treble crochet as an example, after the first row is complete you need to miss a stitch at the beginning of the next and subsequent rows, once you have completed the three turning chains. When you get to the end of the row, you need to find an extra stitch, which you make into the last chain of the turning chain that was made at the beginning of the previous row.

Failing to do these two things will result in an uneven edge.

Counting stitches

When counting the stitches on the final row of your crochet you can count the horizontal chain that runs along the top of them because one chain belongs to each stitch of the row. If you have worked a turning chain at the beginning of the row this will count as one stitch too, so remember to include this even though it might not look like it has a chain sitting horizontally at the top.

For stitches with longer vertical posts, such as treble and double treble crochet, you can count the posts of the stitches. Remember, if you started with a turning chain this will count as a stitch too.

If you want to count stitches on a row that is not your final one, and you therefore cannot see the chain along the top, you will need to identify the posts of the stitches and count those.

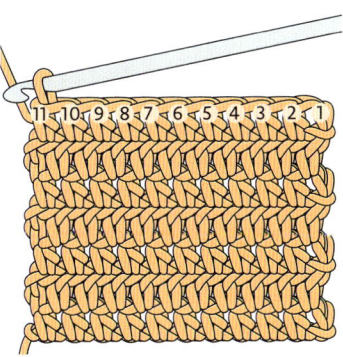
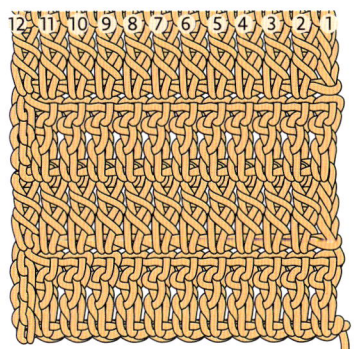

Stitch spaces

A stitch space (st-sp) is the gap that sits between a pair of stitches. A stitch space is easier to identify when the vertical posts of the stitches are relatively tall. Placing a new stitch in a stitch space will make the gap between the stitches wider.

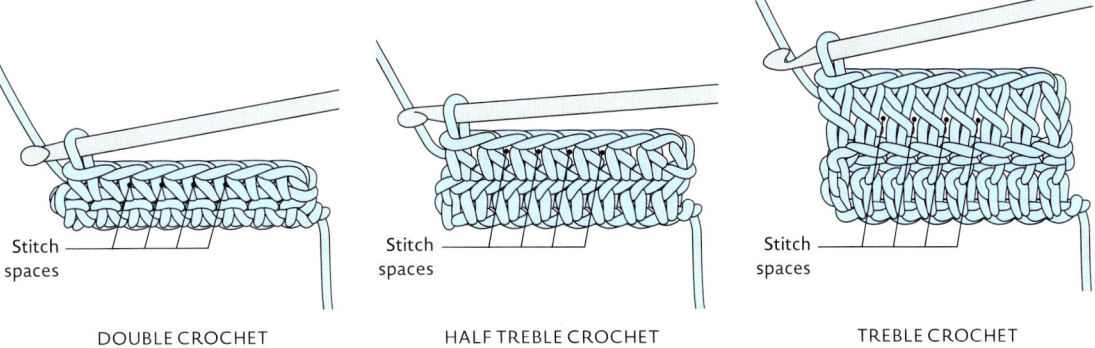

Stitch spaces

Stitch spaces

Stitch spaces

DOUBLE CROCHET

HALF TREBLE CROCHET

TREBLE CROCHET

Increasing and decreasing

There will be places within your crochet projects where you will need to increase your stitch count to make your item bigger, or when you need to decrease the count to make it smaller.

Increasing

The most common way to increase a stitch count is to work more than one stitch into the same place. This could be into a stitch or into a chain space made on a previous row. Working two or three stitches into the same place is a simple increase that does not distort the stitches too much and is therefore not too obvious within the crochet fabric. You can increase midway through a row or you can do so on the first and last stitches when working in rows to create a shaped edge.

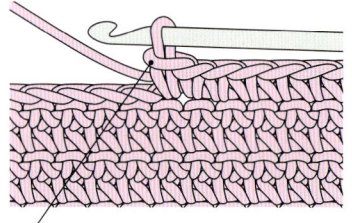

MID ROW DC
You can work two double crochet into the same stitch midway along the row.

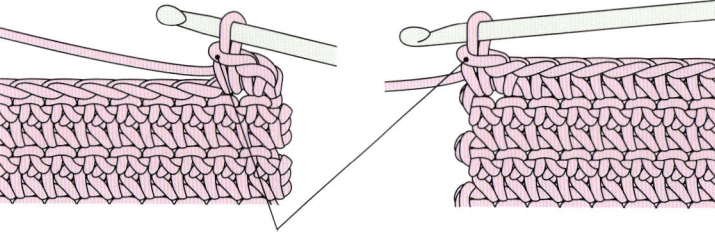

FIRST AND LAST DC
Another method is to work two double crochet into the first and last stitch of a row.

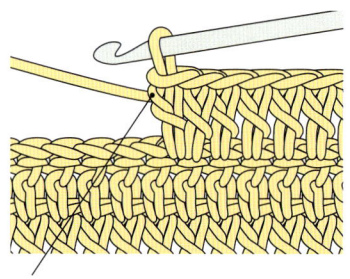

MID ROW TR
You can work two treble crochet into the same stitch midway along the row.

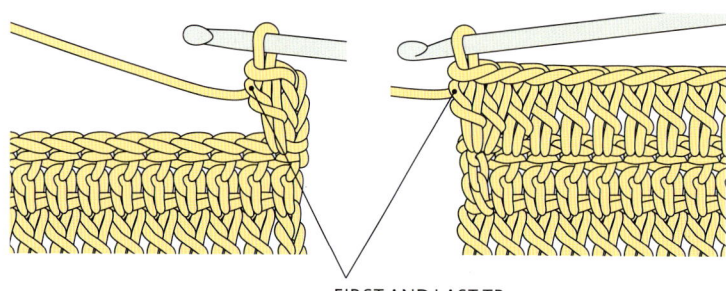

FIRST AND LAST TR
Another method is to work two treble crochet into the first and last stitch of a row.

Jane says

You can work more than a single stitch into the same place, however, when increasing by many stitches, for example four or five, you might need to spread the increases over more stitches: a large increase in one place can distort the fabric.

Decreasing

As a rule, to decrease a stitch count you need to work over a couple of stitches, usually two or three, by creating incomplete stitch posts through each stitch that are drawn together on the final step of the stitch to form one stitch.

DOUBLE CROCHET TWO TOGETHER (DC2TOG)

 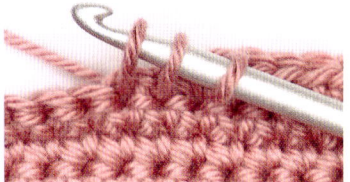 

1   Crochet to the point where you need to make a decrease. Insert the hook into the next stitch and draw a yarn loop through so that there are two loops on the hook.

2   Insert the hook into the next stitch and draw through a yarn loop so that there are three loops on the hook.

3   Catch the yarn and draw it through all three yarn loops to complete the stitch.

DOUBLE CROCHET THREE TOGETHER (DC3TOG)

1   Follow Step 1 of Double Crochet Two Together (DC2TOG). Insert the hook into the next stitch and draw through a yarn loop so that there are three loops on the hook.

2   Insert the hook into the next stitch and draw through a yarn loop so that there are four loops on the hook.

3   Catch the yarn and draw it through all four yarn loops to complete the stitch.

TREBLE CROCHET TWO TOGETHER (TR2TOG)

1 Crochet to the point where you need to make a decrease. Wrap the yarn around the hook and insert it into the next stitch. Draw a yarn loop through so that there are three loops on the hook.

2 Work the first step of a treble crochet stitch by drawing the yarn through two yarn loops on the hook. You will see the first part of the stitch post is made.

3 Wrap the yarn round the hook and insert it into the next stitch. Work the first step of this stitch by drawing the yarn through two yarn loops on the hook. You will see the first part of the second stitch post is made, and there are three loops on the hook.

4 Catch the yarn and draw it through all three yarn loops to complete the stitch.

TREBLE CROCHET THREE TOGETHER (TR3TOG)

1 Follow Steps 1–2 of Treble Crochet Two Together (TR2TOG).

2 Repeat Step 2 of Treble Crochet Two Together (TR2TOG) into the next stitch so that there are four loops on the hook.

3 Catch the yarn and draw it through all four yarn loops to complete the stitch.

Working in rows

When working repeated crochet stitches along a chain or along stitches already made, the sequence of stitches will usually count as a row. When working from a written crochet pattern, this will be written as Row 1, Row 2, Row 3 and so on.

When you work in rows you need to turn your crochet at the end of each row to work the next row. This is like turning the page of a book, in that you simply turn your work over, being careful not to overtwist the loop that remains on the hook as you do so.

Crochet stitches look different on the front to how they do on the back, and rows are often listed in a pattern as being a right-side row (RS) or a wrong-side row (WS).

Counting rows

When working through a crochet pattern you need to keep track of the row you are on to ensure your completed project looks as it should. If you are a beginner, counting rows can be a little tricky. You could use a pencil and paper to mark down rows as you complete them, or use stitch markers placed at the end of a sequence of rows to help guide you.

To count rows you need to recognize the appearance of the stitch you are counting, so if necessary refer back to The Anatomy of a Stitch on pages 45–47.

Jane says

Crochet patterns are written in a standard way, usually with the instruction to make a certain number of turning chains given at the beginning of a row. I find it much easier to make the chain before turning the work for the next row. Working in this way means I can easily identify where to put my hook for the next stitch on the following row.

How to recognize the front and the back of the work

When turning your work at the end of each row your crochet fabric will look almost identical on both sides. A really easy way to know whether you have the right side of your work facing you is to make a note right at the beginning of what side of the work the tail end of yarn is.

As a rule, if you are working right-handed and the tail is on your left, you have the right side (RS) facing you. Vice versa if you are working left-handed.

If you are working right-handed and the tail is on your right, you have the wrong side (WS) facing you. Vice versa if working left-handed.

SEE ALSO
Crochet Stitches, pages 38–44
Increasing and Decreasing, pages 48–50
The Anatomy of a Stitch, pages 45–47

Counting rows created by turning your work

When working in rows the right side of the work will be facing you on one row and the wrong side will be facing you on the next, therefore your crochet forms a pattern based on working alternate rows. Counting your rows in pairs can make it easier once you are able to recognize the sequence.

Total row count is 26 rows.

The sample is made using an even number of rows, so the final row is a wrong-side row.

Here the row count is eight rows.

Here the row count is six rows.

Here the row count is four rows.

Two sets of two rows, using blue then pink yarn.

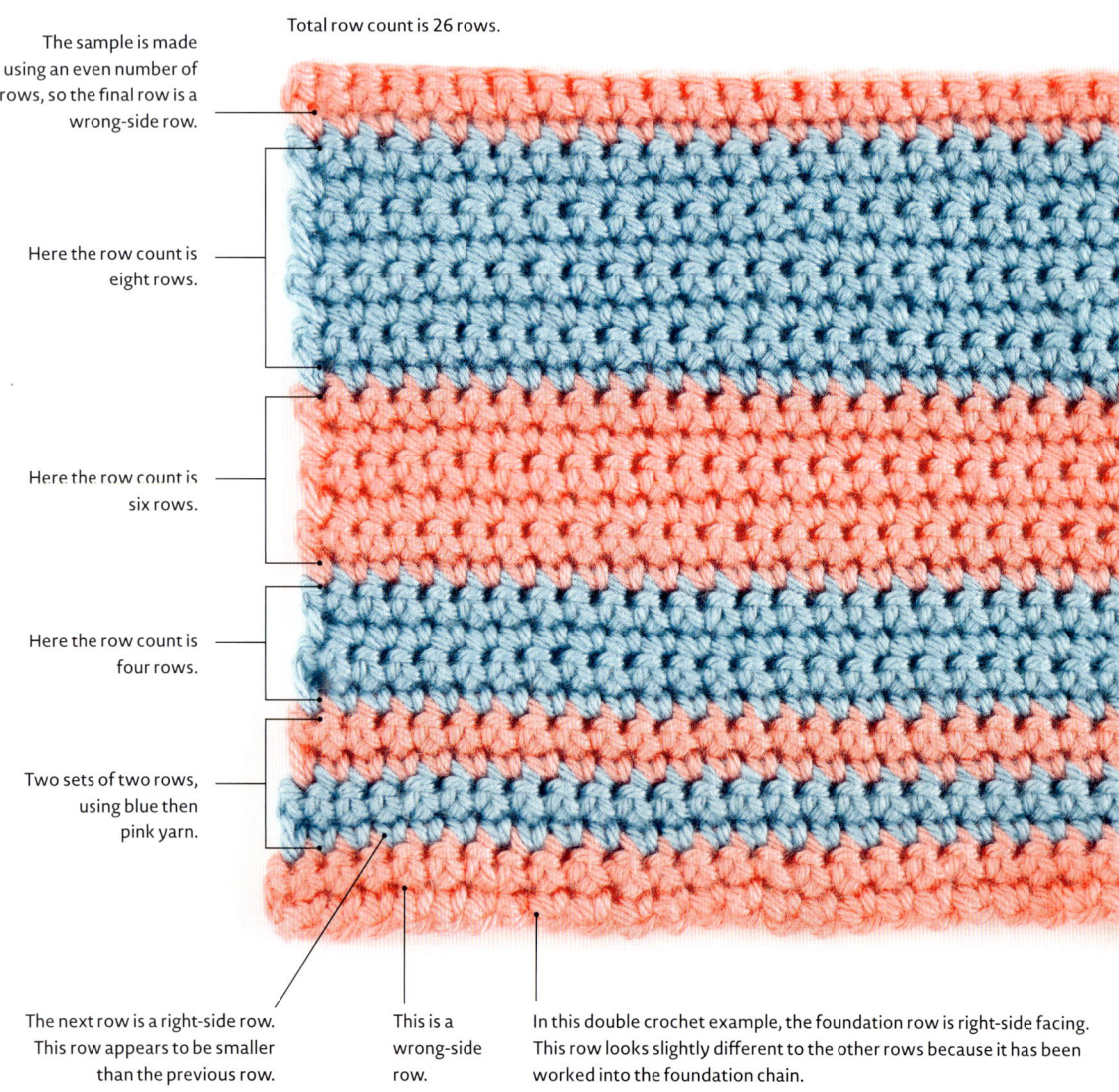

The next row is a right-side row. This row appears to be smaller than the previous row.

This is a wrong-side row.

In this double crochet example, the foundation row is right-side facing. This row looks slightly different to the other rows because it has been worked into the foundation chain.

Working in the round

As well as working in rows, crochet can be worked in rounds. As a rule, rounds are worked with the right side facing you, so the work is not routinely turned. Rows of crochet will look different when worked in the round compared to how they look when your work is turned. When working in this way a written pattern would refer to rounds rather than rows, for example Round 1, Round 2 and so on.

To follow a chart for a motif worked in the round (see pages 32–33), start from the centre and work outward towards the final round. At the central point the chart will show the number of chains you need to make the foundation ring.

What is a motif?

A motif is a piece of crochet, usually worked in the round, to any shape and size, that can be joined to another identical or similar piece to create a larger project, such as an item of clothing or an afghan. The most common crochet motif is probably the traditional granny square (see page 70), but the word motif can be applied to myriad crochet pieces. A motif is likely to be worked in such a way that it stays relatively flat rather than creating a tube (see pages 61–62).

SEE ALSO

Slip stitches

When working in the round, a slip stitch (ss) is used to finish a round and produce a neat join where the first and last stitches meet. It has little height and looks like a chain stitch, so it can also be used to help you travel from one point in your work to another.

1 Insert the hook under the chain that sits at the top of the next stitch.

2 Draw the yarn through the stitch with the hook.

Making a neat foundation ring

When working in the round, the most common first step is to make a foundation ring. This is a series of chains joined by a slip stitch to form a ring. Since the ring sits at the centre of the motif it is important that you make it as neat as possible.

1 Make the required number of chains. Insert the hook into the first chain you made – the one after the slipknot. It doesn't matter whether you insert the hook so that you have one yarn loop on it or two.

2 Move the tail end of yarn over the hook so that the slipknot moves over the hook to your right side (left if you are left-handed).

3 Making sure that the tail end stays in place so that the slipknot has moved over the hook, catch the ball end of yarn and draw through the chain and yarn loop on the hook to complete.

4 Use your fingers to open up the centre of the ring so that you can clearly see where to place your stitches.

Working into the foundation ring

You now work your stitches into the centre of the foundation ring. If the ring is relatively small you might need to use your fingers or hook to stretch it open a little.

You can work any stitch into a ring. This example shows treble crochet, so the yarn is wrapped around the hook before making each stitch.

MESSY RING
You can see part of the slipknot at the front of the work because the tail end of yarn has not been moved to the back.

NEAT RING

1 Make three chains (this counts as the first stitch).

2 Wrap the yarn round the hook. Insert the hook into the centre of the ring and complete the stitch in the usual way.

3 Continuing to work into the centre of the ring, work half the required number of stitches and push them around the ring so that the remaining half is visible. This will ensure all stitches fit into the ring.

4 Complete the remaining stitches to fill the ring.

5 Work a slip stitch to join.

Formula for increases

The stitch count increases row by row when working a motif in the round. Imagine a slice of cake, cut from a larger, round cake. The piece is tiny at its tip, where it was cut from the centre of the cake, and gets wider towards its outside edge. Now think of a crochet motif in relation to the piece of cake. The motif is tiny at the centre, but becomes bigger (and therefore the stitch count increases) as the motif is worked.

A pattern will instruct you on increasing, but if you want to make your own motif in the round there is a standard formula for increases, but before you start you do need to think about what shape you are ultimately aiming to achieve, and whether you have specific stitch repeats to accommodate within the piece.

The following formula is based on a treble crochet circular motif:

- **FOUNDATION RING:** Start with a chain and form a ring with a slip stitch.

  Before you make the chain , decide how many stitches you want the ring to accommodate on the foundation round. As a rule, the chain should be half this number. For example, if the next round needs 12 stitches make a six-chain ring. When making a large motif you may find you need fewer chains. The same applies when dealing with odd numbers.

- **FOUNDATION ROUND:** Once you have made the ring, work three chains (to count as your first treble crochet stitch) then work the remaining stitches into the ring, ending with a slip stitch to join.

  For this example, when working into the six-chain ring you will need a stitch count of 12 stitches.

- **ROUND 1:** Double the stitch count.

  To double the stitch count work two stitches into each stitch. In line with the example, this would take the stitch count to 24 stitches.

- **ROUND 2:** Increase into every alternate stitch (which also means you will increase by the number of stitches you originally started with).

  In line with the example this is an increase of 12 stitches, so you would work two stitches into one stitch and one stitch into the next stitch, then repeat the sequence for the whole round.

- **ROUND 3:** Increase by one stitch in every three stitches (which again means you will increase by the number of stitches you originally started with).

  In line with the example this is an increase of another 12 stitches, working two stitches into the next stitch and one stitch into each of the next two stitches. Repeat the sequence for the whole round.

- **ROUND 4:** Increase by one stitch in every four stitches (which again means you will increase by the number of stitches you originally started with).

  In line with the example this is an increase of 12 stitches, so you would work two stitches into the next stitch and one stitch into each of the next three stitches. Repeat the sequence for the whole round.

- On the following rounds continue to place the increases as set by the last few rounds with the stitch count between increases getting larger by one stitch on every subsequent round.

  In line with the example, the stitch count on every round will increase by 12 stitches (12 being the initial stitch count achieved on the foundation round).

Stitch counts based on this example:
Foundation ring: 6ch
Foundation round: 12sts
Round 1: 24sts
Round 2: 36sts
Round 3: 48sts
Round 4: 60sts
Round 5: 72sts
Round 6: 84sts

TROUBLESHOOTING

It is as important to achieve the correct tension when working in the round as it is when working in rows. If you achieve the wrong tension you may find that your motif becomes cupped or wavy.

Cupped If your motif is cupped, and you have created the correct number of stitches, you are working too tightly. Try using a larger size hook.

Wavy If the motif is wavy, and you have created the correct number of stitches, you are working too loosely. Try using a smaller size hook.

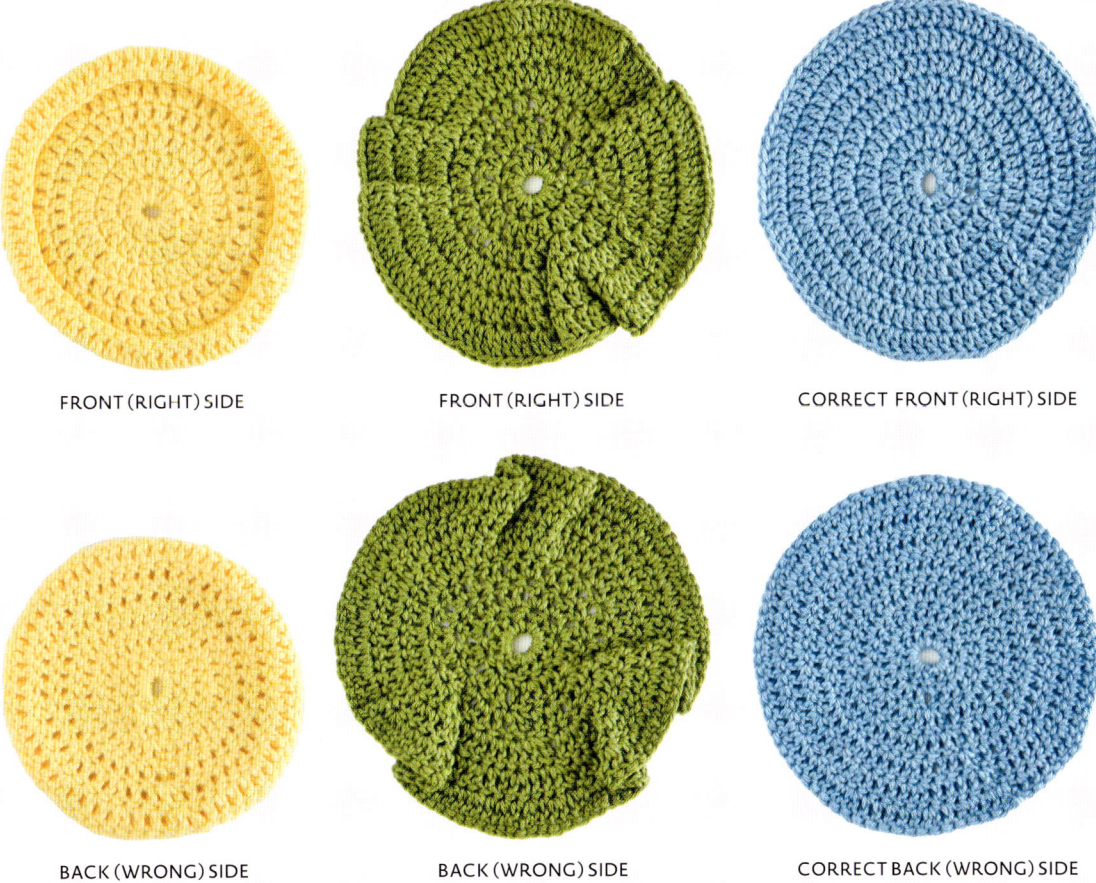

FRONT (RIGHT) SIDE FRONT (RIGHT) SIDE CORRECT FRONT (RIGHT) SIDE

BACK (WRONG) SIDE BACK (WRONG) SIDE CORRECT BACK (WRONG) SIDE

Own design If you have created your own design and it becomes cupped or wavy you may need to amend the stitch count. If your tension is correct but your motif is cupped this suggests you do not have enough stitches so you might need to add some extra. If your motif is wavy this suggests you have too many stitches and may need to work fewer.

A neat join for the final round

When you fasten off the yarn in the usual way when working in the round, the slip-stitch join does not look the same as the top of the other stitches on the round. This doesn't matter when you are working lots of rounds, but might look obvious on the final round when there is no subsequent round to cover the join.

I use two techniques for making a neater join: using a hook when working subsequent rows, then using a tapestry needle on the final round.

USING A HOOK

1 When working a stitch with a longer post, such as half treble crochet or treble crochet, insert the hook through the last chain at the top of the turning chain made at the beginning of the round, from back to front.

2 Wrap the yarn around the hook and draw through to the front of the work.

3 Cut the yarn end and gently draw through the stitch to the front.

4 From the back, insert the hook through the same stitch and wrap the tail of yarn around the hook.

5 Draw the yarn through to the reverse of the work. Sew in the tail end.

GOOD JOIN

BAD JOIN
If you make an extra chain before fastening off the yarn it will create a slight bump on the outside edge of your work.

USING A TAPESTRY NEEDLE

1 Making sure it doesn't unravel, gently remove the hook from the yarn loop made by the last stitch. Cut the yarn end and gently pull the yarn loop so that the tail end feeds all the way through it.

2 Thread the yarn end through the eye of a large needle. Sew the yarn around the top of the first stitch of the round to mimic the horizontal chain stitch.

3 Sew the yarn through the chain at the top of the last stitch of the row from front to back and tighten gently.

SEWN JOIN
I like to finish the final round with a sewn join, but you can use a hook if you prefer.

4 Sew in the yarn end at the back of the work.

RIGHT AND WRONG SIDE

When working in the round to create a flat motif, especially when making more complicated designs, it can be difficult to decipher the front from the back of the work. As a rule, the front (right side) of the work has a smoother appearance to the reverse side (wrong side).

Jane says

Here we show the join made using treble crochet. When working double crochet, insert the hook through the chain at the top of the stitch at the beginning of the round rather than into the third chain.

Counting rounds

Counting rounds on a motif can be quite tricky, especially if the crochet is decorative. If the piece is simple you should be able to recognize the rounds, but you need to keep in mind that all rounds will be right-side facing, so you will only see the front posts of the stitches (see The Anatomy of a Stitch, pages 45–47).

When looking at a more complicated motif you might want to look for the place where the rounds start and finish. Adding markers into the joins will help you count.

How to avoid a motif becoming biased

Crochet stitches form an offset brick pattern, so when working motifs that are made with the right side facing throughout, the place where a round finishes appears to move across by one stitch on every round. This probably won't be noticeable when making a motif without corners, such as a simple circle, flower or mandala. However, when working a motif with corners, such as a granny square, it can start to look like it has become biased.

To combat this you can work some of the rounds with the wrong side facing.

RIGHT-SIDE FACING
This granny square has been worked with the right-side facing throughout, and has become a little biased.

ALTERNATE ROWS
When making this granny square the work was turned every alternate round, so it remains square.

Jane says

When working in the round, especially when using a high number of stitches, you might find yourself accidentally switching between right and wrong sides of the work. Place a stitch marker on the right side of the work so you can easily differentiate between sides.

Tubular crochet

You can work crochet in the round to create tubular fabric, a technique that is used to great effect to make stuffed toys, such as the Japanese-inspired amigurumi. These toys are filled with soft stuffing that could spill out of crochet holes, so they are traditionally made in the round to a very tight tension.

Magic ring

A magic ring (also known as a magic loop or a base ring) can be made in place of a series of chains to create the ring at the centre of a motif worked in the round. The magic ring allows you to tighten the centre of your motif so no hole remains, and works best if you only have a small number of stitches on your first round of crochet.

A magic ring is a loose slipknot that is worked into before tightening.

PULL TO TIGHTEN
You need to make the magic-ring slipknot in a specific way, so that when you pull the yarn tail the hole will tighten.

SEE ALSO

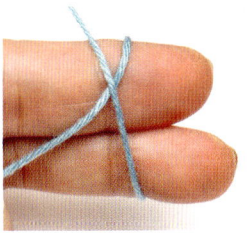

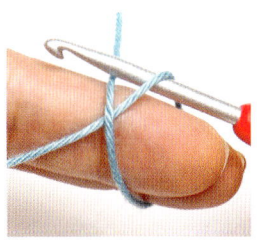

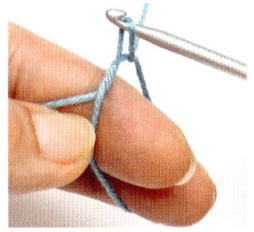

1 Anchoring the tail end of yarn within your hand, take the yarn over two fingers from front to back, making sure that the yarn crosses over to create a yarn loop. Hold the tension of the loop with your thumb.

2 With the hook facing downwards, insert it through the loop on your hand. Catch the ball end of yarn into the crook of the hook.

3 Rotating the hook to catch the yarn loop, draw through the yarn loop on your fingers so that you have a loop on the hook. This is the equivalent of an untightened slipknot.

4 Carefully remove the yarn loops from your fingers, making sure not to twist anything. The tail end of yarn should be on your left-hand side if you are right-handed and on your right-hand side if you are left-handed.

5 Holding the yarn loop open so that it doesn't tighten, make one chain.

6 Work the required number of stitches into the loop, working over the yarn that makes the loop and the tail end at the same time. Pull the tail end of yarn to tighten.

Counting tubular rounds

When you work in the round to create a tube of crochet you will probably work with the right side facing you most of the time. This means that you will see the front side of the stitches on most rounds – as opposed to seeing alternate wrong sides as you do when working turned rows. This means that a crochet fabric worked in the round will look different to that worked in rows, even when they are both made using the same stitch.

When working in this way it is imperative that you keep counting your stitches and rounds. Use stitch markers to help you do this and make a note of numbers every couple of rounds. Try to make it a habit to place a locking stitch marker on the last stitch you make as you work each round. When you work your final stitch into the marked stitch move the marker into the new stitch.

Total round count is 26 rounds.

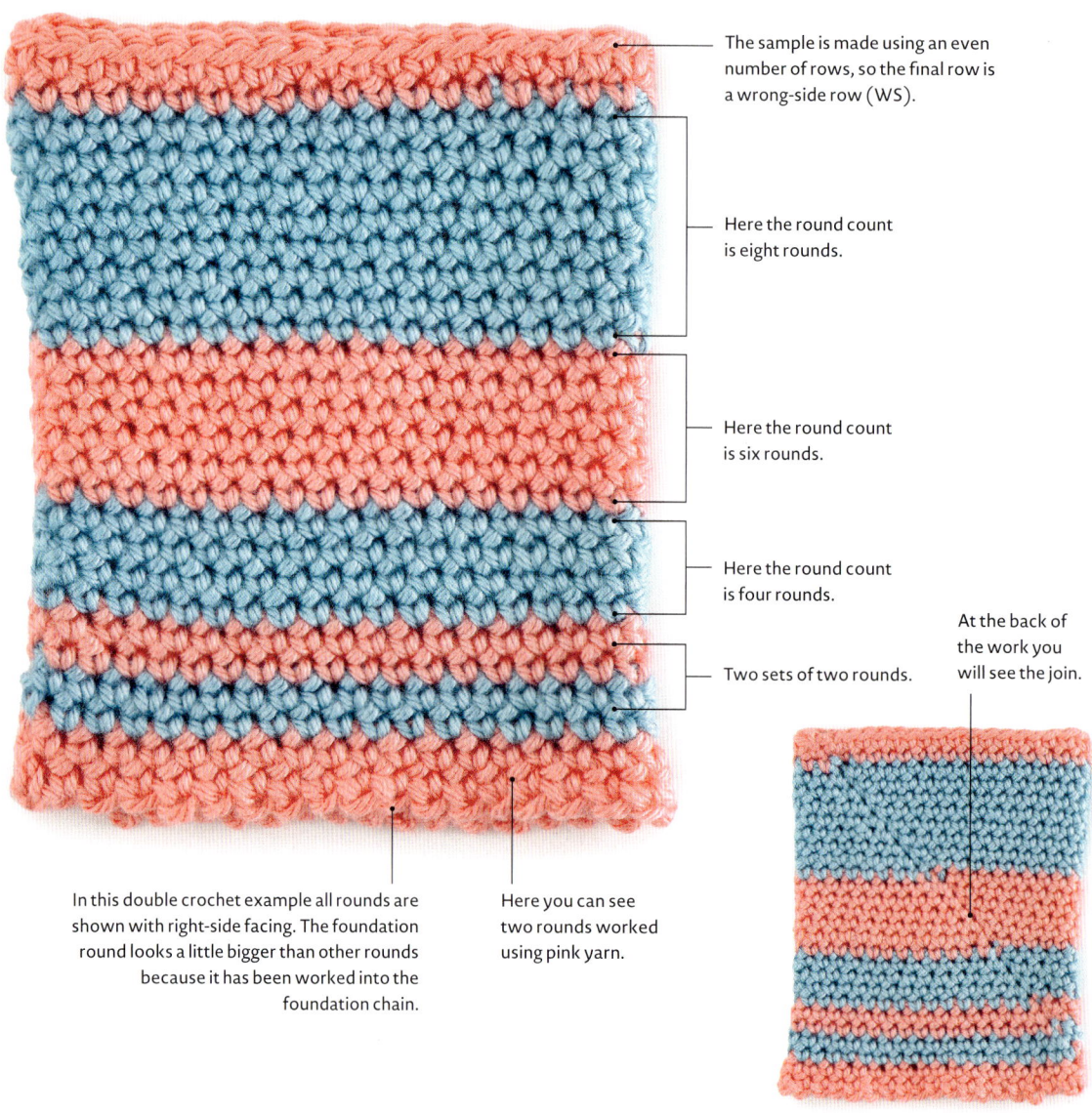

The sample is made using an even number of rows, so the final row is a wrong-side row (WS).

Here the round count is eight rounds.

Here the round count is six rounds.

Here the round count is four rounds.

Two sets of two rounds.

At the back of the work you will see the join.

In this double crochet example all rounds are shown with right-side facing. The foundation round looks a little bigger than other rounds because it has been worked into the foundation chain.

Here you can see two rounds worked using pink yarn.

Joining in a new yarn

Once you have completed a crochet stitch you will be left with a yarn loop on the hook. When changing yarn shade, either at the beginning of a row or round or midway, this yarn loop can create a messy colour change. To achieve a neat change, plan how you will join in the new yarn, using one of the techniques shown here.

Round joining techniques

You will achieve a much neater yarn change if you complete rounds and fasten off the yarn, rather than joining mid-stitch. Aim to join the new yarn in a position away from where you fastened off the previous one, so that yarn ends do not all end up in the same place.

Jane says

A slip stitch made for the join can look like a stitch when you are working the following round, so make sure you count correctly and do not count the slip stitch as a stitch when working subsequent rounds.

JOINING THE YARN IN DOUBLE CROCHET

1 Insert the hook through the stitch where you want to join in the new yarn and use the hook to draw the yarn through the stitch.

2 Make one chain.

3 Work a double crochet stitch into the same place.

4 This process can make it look like you have two stitches at the base of the stitch, so use your fingers to gently pull the yarn tail through the stitch.

SEE ALSO

Crochet Stitches, pages 38–44

Working in Rows, pages 51–52

Working in the Round, pages 53–60

JOINING THE YARN IN TREBLE CROCHET

1 Insert the hook through the stitch where you want to join in the new yarn and use the hook to draw the yarn through the stitch.

2 Make one chain. Place the tail end of yarn over the chain.

3 Make another chain to secure the yarn tail.

4 Make another chain to create the final chain of the turning chain.

MESSY JOIN
If you consistently change yarn shade at the same point in your work, it will create the effect of a scar that runs through each row.

NEAT JOIN
If you fasten off at the end of a row and join the new yarn in at a different point on the next row you will achieve a neat join.

STANDING STITCHES FOR TREBLE CROCHET

When working treble crochet you might prefer that the chains created to act as a turning chain look the same as a stitch, in which case, you can try this method.

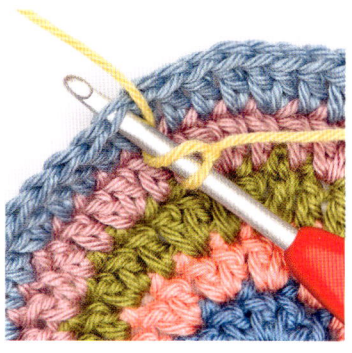

1 Place a slipknot on the hook and keep hold of the yarn tail. Wrap the yarn around the hook so that two yarn loops are on the hook.

2 Keeping the yarn loops on the hook, insert the hook into the stitch.

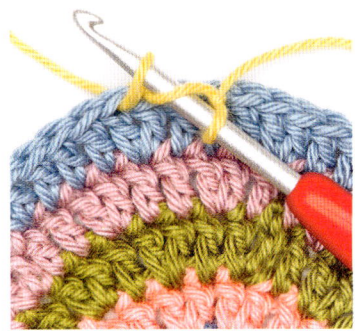

3 Wrap the yarn around the hook and draw through the stitch so that there are three loops on the hook. You will need to hold the tension on the tail end of yarn as you do this.

4 Catch the yarn again and draw through two yarn loops on the hook.

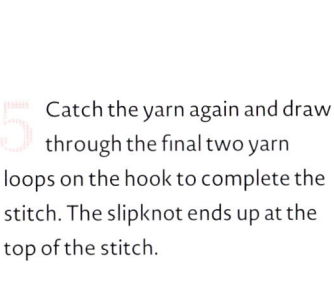

5 Catch the yarn again and draw through the final two yarn loops on the hook to complete the stitch. The slipknot ends up at the top of the stitch.

End of row joining techniques

When working double crochet you can change yarn at the end of a row, in which case the method is the same whether you have the right or wrong side of the work facing you.

To change yarn midway along a row, if the right side of the work is facing you, use the same techniques as for the end of a row. To change yarn on a wrong-side row follow the steps for Double Crochet Midway Wrong Side.

DOUBLE CROCHET END OF ROW

1 Work the double crochet stitch to the point where you have just one action needed to complete the stitch, so that two yarn loops are on the hook.

2 Keeping the tail ends of yarn tight so that they don't become loose, draw the new yarn through the yarn loops on the hook to complete the stitch.

DOUBLE CROCHET MIDWAY WRONG SIDE

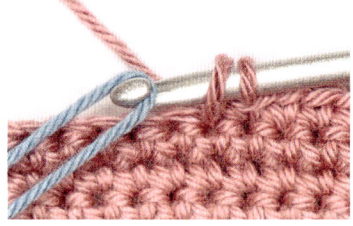

1 Work the double crochet stitch to the point where you have just one action needed to complete the stitch, so two yarn loops are left on the hook.

2 Keeping the tail ends of yarn tight so that they don't become loose, lay the new yarn over the work and hold as usual.

3 Draw the new yarn through the yarn loops on the hook to complete the stitch.

STITCHES WITH LONGER POSTS

When working stitches with longer posts, such as treble or double treble crochet, you will need to complete all the steps of the stitch except the final one, before changing yarn shade following the steps for Double Crochet Midway Wrong Side.

In the case of treble crochet this means that you will have completed the first part of the post of the stitch before changing yarn shade.

Frogging

To avoid making mistakes in the first place, you need to constantly check your work, both the right and wrong sides, since it is easy to get so wrapped up in the action of crocheting that you don't notice an error. Probably the most common mistake is achieving an incorrect stitch count.

Because of the nature of crochet, you cannot unravel just one stitch and correct it like you can when handknitting. A mistake made early on in your work can only be rectified by unravelling the rows, correcting the error, then reworking the crochet. This process is often referred to as frogging.

If you find you are losing a stitch on every row or round, remind yourself of where to work your first and last stitches and whether your turning chains count as a stitch.

> ### Jane says
>
> The action of frogging can cause the yarn you have unravelled to become stretched or uneven, so that when you re-crochet them the rows may not match the previous ones. My advice is to cut away the used yarn and join in a new yarn end so that it yarn matches perfectly.

Cutting instead of unravelling

When working stitches with longer posts, such as treble crochet and double treble crochet, you can cut through a row with scissors instead of unravelling the yarn. This is probably quicker than unravelling row by row – for example, if you have made many rows after the mistake – but you need to be sure you have enough room to cut through the centre point of all the stitches, and that you are able to cut straight.

Once you have cut through the crochet you can unravel the row that has been cut by gently pulling out all loose yarn ends. To one side of the cut you will see the chain that runs along the top of the previous row. Once you unravel to this point you can rejoin your yarn and continue to crochet.

Shapes and stitches

ONCE YOU HAVE GOT TO GRIPS WITH THE BASIC
CROCHET STITCHES, YOU CAN MAKE LOTS OF DIFFERENT
PATTERNS BY USING THEM IN VARIOUS COMBINATIONS.
INTRODUCE SMALL ADAPTATIONS TO YOUR STITCHES
AND YOU CAN CREATE SHAPES, TEXTURES
AND PRETTY DECORATIVE EFFECTS.

Creating shapes

One of the fabulous things about crochet is that you can create motifs in all sorts of shapes and sizes. These can be flat or three-dimensional, and can take pretty much any form.

Motifs with straight sides, such as squares, triangles and hexagons, are probably the most common shapes created in crochet. Fitting smaller shapes together to create a patchwork-type fabric is a typical way of making larger projects.

The traditional granny square is what people invariably picture when they think of crochet, so it is not surprising that making one is considered one of the first 'rites of passage' for any new crocheter. A traditional granny square is made using a different shade of yarn per round, but squares can also be made in one colour.

The way that traditional granny shapes are made is similar regardless of the shape you are creating, which means you can use the same techniques to stitch triangles and hexagons.

Traditional granny square

Using your first choice of yarn shade, make 6 ch and join with a ss to form a ring.

Round 1 (RS): 3 ch (counts as 1 tr), 2 tr into ring, 3 ch, [3 tr, 3 ch into ring, 3 ch] 3 times, ss to join, fasten off, turn (12 sts & 4 ch-sps).

Round 2 (WS): Using the next shade, join yarn into any 3 ch-sp by working 1 ch, make 2 more chain (counts as 1 tr), [2 tr, 3 ch, 3 tr into same ch-sp], 1 ch, * [3 tr, 3 ch, 3 tr] into next ch-sp, 1 ch; repeat from * to end, ss to join, fasten off, turn (24 sts & 4 ch-sps).

Round 3 (RS): Using the next shade, join yarn into any 3 ch-sp by working 1 ch, make 2 more chain (counts as 1 tr), [2 tr, 3 ch, 3 tr into same ch-sp], 1 ch, 3 tr into next ch-sp, 1 ch, * [3 tr, 3 ch, 3 tr] into next ch-sp, 1 ch, 3 tr into next ch-sp,

1 ch; repeat from * to end, ss to join, fasten off, turn (36 sts & 8 ch-sps).

Round 4 (WS): Using the next shade, join yarn into any 3 ch-sp by working 1 ch, make 2 more chain (counts as 1 tr), [2 tr, 3 ch, 3 tr into same ch-sp], [1 ch, 3 tr into next ch-sp, 1ch] twice, * [3 tr, 3 ch, 3 tr] into next ch-sp, [1 ch, 3 tr into next ch-sp, 1ch] twice; repeat from * to end, ss to join, fasten off, turn (48 sts & 8 ch-sps).

To make the granny square larger, continue to work as set, simply adding more blocks of three stitches into one chain space made between each corner on every round. The size of a granny square worked in this way is infinite.

SEE ALSO

Granny triangle

Using your fir st choice of yarn shade make 4 ch and join with a ss to form a ring.

Round 1 (RS): 3 ch (counts as 1 tr), 2 tr into ring, 3 ch, [3 tr, 3 ch into ring, 3 ch] twice, ss to join, fasten off, turn (9 sts & 3 ch-sps).

Round 2 (WS): using the next shade, join yarn into any 3 ch-sp by working 1 ch, make 2 more chain (counts as 1 tr), [2 tr, 3 ch, 3 tr into same ch-sp], 1 ch, * [3 tr, 3 ch, 3 tr] into next ch-sp, 1 ch; repeat from * to end, ss to join, fasten off, turn (18 sts & 3 ch-sps).

Round 3 (RS): using the next shade, join yarn into any 3 ch-sp by working 1 ch, make 2 more chain (counts as 1 tr), [2 tr, 3 ch, 3 tr into same ch-sp], 1 ch, 3 tr into next ch-sp, 1 ch, * [3 tr, 3 ch, 3 tr] into next ch-sp, 1 ch, 3 tr into next ch-sp, 1 ch; repeat from * to end, ss to join, fasten off, turn (27 sts & 6 ch-sps).

Round 4 (WS): using the next shade, join yarn into any 3 ch-sp by working 1 ch, make 2 more chain (counts as 1 tr), [2 tr, 3 ch, 3 tr into same ch-sp], [1 ch, 3 tr into next ch-sp, 1 ch] twice, * [3 tr, 3 ch, 3 tr] into next ch-sp, [1 ch, 3 tr into next ch-sp, 1 ch] twice; repeat from * to end, ss to join, fasten off, turn (36 sts & 9 ch-sps).

To make the granny triangle larger, continue to work as set, simply adding more blocks of three stitches into one chain space made between each corner on every round. The size of a granny triangle worked in this way is infinite.

Jane says

If you continuously work with the right side of the work facing you when crocheting in the round to create shapes and corners, you may find that your work becomes biased (see page 60). Turning at the end of each row so that you are working with alternate sides facing you will combat this.

DO THE MATHS

To make a simple motif in a shape other than a circle, think about the number of stitches needed to create that shape before you start.

- To create a triangle you need a stitch count divisible by three.
- For a square you need a stitch count divisible by four.
- To create a pentagon you need a stitch count divisible by five.
- For a hexagon you need a stitch count divisible by six.
- To create an octagon you need a stitch count divisible by eight.

To create a motif that starts as one shape – such as a circle – and becomes another shape – perhaps an octagon – you need to calculate stitch counts that will work mathematically for both shapes.

Jane says

If you find you have got your maths wrong or change your mind about the shape you want to make, you can alter the stitch counts a little to make things work. To do this you may need to decrease a few stitches or increase more than you thought on one or more rounds.

Granny hexagon

Using your fir st choice of yarn shade make 7 ch and join with a ss to form a ring.

Round 1 (RS): 3 ch (counts as 1 tr), 2 tr into ring, 3 ch, [3 tr, 3 ch into ring, 3 ch] five times, ss to join, fasten off, turn (18 sts & 6 ch-sps).

Round 2 (WS): using the next shade, join yarn into any 3 ch-sp by working 1 ch, make 2 more chain (counts as 1 tr), [2 tr, 3 ch, 3 tr into same ch-sp], 1 ch, * [3 tr, 3 ch, 3 tr] into next ch-sp, 1 ch; repeat from * to end, ss to join, fasten off, turn (36 sts & 12 ch-sps).

Round 3 (RS): using the next shade, join yarn into any 3 ch-sp by working 1 ch, make 2 more chain (counts as 1 tr), [2 tr, 3 ch, 3 tr into same ch-sp], 1 ch, 3 tr into next ch-sp, 1 ch, * [3 tr, 3 ch, 3 tr] into next ch-sp, 1 ch, 3 tr into next ch-sp, 1 ch; repeat from * to end, ss to join, fasten off, turn (54 sts & 18 ch-sps).

Round 4 (WS): using the next shade, join yarn into any 3 ch-sp by working 1 ch, make 2 more chain (counts as 1 tr), [2 tr, 3 ch, 3 tr into same ch-sp], [1 ch, 3 tr into next ch-sp, 1 ch] twice, * [3 tr, 3 ch, 3 tr] into next ch-sp, [1 ch, 3 tr into next ch-sp, 1 ch] twice; repeat from * to end, ss to join, fasten off, turn (72 sts & 24 ch-sps).

To make the granny hexagon larger, continue to work as set, simply adding more blocks of three stit ches into one chain space made between each corner on every round. The size of a hexagon worked in this way is infinite.

Single-colour grannies

To make a single-coloured granny square, triangle or hexagon, work as for the traditional granny shape, but do not fasten off at the end of Round 1.

Instead, work one slip stitch into the top of the next two stitches, then another one into the next three chain spaces. As the yarn will still be attached to the work (which means you do not need to add in a new one) work three chains (counts as one treble crochet) in place of the one chain plus two chains, then follow the pattern from Round 2.

Jane says

When crocheting unusual shapes, I draw the shape to scale on a paper template that I can then compare to my crochet as I work.

Corner techniques

You can create corners in a few different ways.

To create corners over a few rounds – shown here is double crochet – make them by working more than one stitch (three or five is the most common) into one stitch. Do this in the same place over a few rounds to achieve a corner.

Perhaps the most common way to create a corner is by working in line with a traditional granny-square pattern by working 3 tr, 3 ch, 3 tr into the place you want to create the corner. You can do this by working into just one stitch, two consecutive stitches, or a chain space made on a previous round.

To create a gradually sloping corner you can work a variety of stitches with different post lengths. For example, you could choose to work 1 dc, 1 htr, 1 tr, 1 dtr into one stitch, then 1 dtr, 1 tr, 1 htr, 1 tr into the next stitch.

Tessellating shapes

To make motifs that fit together, look at the various ways shapes tessellate. Some fit neatly together themselves, while others need 'filler' shapes in the gaps to create a complete fabric.

Search 'tessellating graph paper' on the internet to find lots of exciting layouts and see just how many shapes can fit together!

Jane says

Some shapes with odd numbers of sides, such as the five-sided pentagon, do not remain flat when joined together, and only tessellate to a three-dimensional shape.

If you want your joined motifs to make a fabric with a straight edge you may need to make half and/or quarter motifs to achieve those edges.

Textural stitches

When working in double or treble crochet it is usual to work under the chain that runs along the top of the previous row. However, you can create interesting textural stitches by working into alternative parts of the stitches.

Working into front and back loops

While you would usually put the hook underneath the whole of the chain that runs along the top of the previous row, to create textural stitch patterns you work into the chain itself. You can choose to work into either the front or back of the chain, so that you are working through only part of the chain, leaving the remaining part visible on either the right or wrong side of the work.

FRONT LOOP
With the right side of the work facing you, insert the hook through the front of the next chain that runs along the top of the work, and make the stitch into the single yarn loop of the chain.

BACK LOOP
Working into the back loop of the chain is a little trickier, because you need to position the crochet so that you can clearly see the chain that runs along the top of the work. Insert the hook into the back of the next chain and make the stitch into the single yarn loop of the chain.

Jane says

When working front and back loop crochet you work into a single yarn strand of the chain, so it can look a little loopy and make you feel like you are stretching the chain. Don't worry, consecutive stitches should even out the tension.

SEE ALSO

Common Pattern Abbreviations, page 138
Crochet Stitches, pages 38–44
The Anatomy of a Stitch, pages 45–47

ALTERNATING ROWS
This fabric has been created by working alternate front and back loop stitches.

Ridge stitches

You can create the effect of a ridge in crochet fabric by working into the back or front loop of a stitch, or by working around the front or back post of the stitches (see page 76). By working a combination of these techniques, you can create effective textural stitches, especially when using half treble crochet, as in the following examples.

For royal ridge stitch, look at the back of your work when working half treble crochet and you will see the chain that runs along the top of the stitches and, underneath that, the yarn that was wrapped around the hook before you started to make the stitch. This creates an extra wrap of yarn below the chain, referred to as the yarn wrap.

> ### Jane says
> Use a larger hook size for all ridge stitching.

ROYAL RIDGE STITCH

This stitch can be made over any number of stitches.

Make the chain to the required number adding 1 tch.
Foundation row: miss next ch, 1 htr into each ch to end, turn.
Row 1 (RS): 1 ch (does not count as a st), 1 htr into the yarn wrap behind the first stitch directly below the 1 ch, 1 htr into each yarn wrap to end, working the final stitch into the turning chain, turn.
Row 2 (WS): work as row 1.
Repeat as set by row 1 and row 2, working into the yarn wraps at the back of every stitch to desired length.

OPEN RIDGE STITCH

One row is worked around the post and the next row into the back loop. The stitch is made over a repeat of an odd number of stitches.

Make the chain to the required number adding 1 tch.
Foundation row: miss 1 ch, 1dc into next ch, 1 dc into each ch to end, turn.
Row 1 (RS): 2 ch (counts as htr), miss st at base of 2-ch, 1 htr into next st * miss next stitch, 1 htr into next st, work the next htr into the chain space you have just created by working around the post of the last htr you made; repeat from * to last st, 1 htr into next st, turn.
Row 2 (WS): 1 ch (does not count as a st), 1 dc into back loop of st at base of 1-ch, 1 dc into back loop of each st to end, working final st into tch, turn.
Repeat as set by row 1 and row 2 to desired length.

ALMOND RIDGE STITCH

Make a chain divisible by 8 + 5.
Row 1 (RS): miss 1 ch, 1 ss into each next 4 sts, [1 htr into each next 4 sts, 1 ss into each next 4 sts] to end, turn.
Row 2 (WS): 1 ch (does not count as a st), working all sts into back loop 1 ss into st at base of 1 ch, 1 ss into each next 3 sts, [1 htr into each next 4 sts, 1 ss into each next 4 sts] to end, turn.
Row 3 (RS): 2 ch (counts as 1 htr), miss st at base of 2-ch, working all sts into back loop 1 htr into each next 3 sts, [1 ss into each next 4 sts, 1 htr into each next 4 sts] to end, turn.
Row 4 (WS): work as for row 3, turn.
Row 5 (RS): work as row 2 working final st into tch, turn.
Work as set, repeating row 2 through to row 5 to desired length.

Working around the post

Working around the post of a stitch creates a ridge in the work.

Instead of working underneath the next chain at the top of the previous row to create a new stitch, you can create a back post (BP) or front post (FP) stitch by working into two chains, starting by inserting the hook into the stitch either from the front (as usual) or from the back.

DOUBLE CROCHET FRONT POST

1 Insert the hook into the next stitch in the usual way, so that the hook goes under the next chain from front to back.

2 From this position bring the hook through the next stitch along from the back to the front, so that the hook has been into two chain stitches and you can see the post of the stitch on the front of the hook.

3 Complete the stitch in the usual way.

4 You will notice that the chain that runs along the top of the work is visible on the wrong side of the work.

FRONT POST
In this example the textured stitch has been made in the original stitch colour, however, for clarity, a second colour of yarn has been used in the steps.

5 To work the next stitch, insert the hook into the same place that the second part of the last stitch was worked (so that in effect the chain is used twice). From this position bring the hook through the next stitch along from the back to the front so that it has been into two chain stitches and you can see the post of the stitch on the front of the hook. Complete the stitch in the usual way.

DOUBLE CROCHET BACK POST

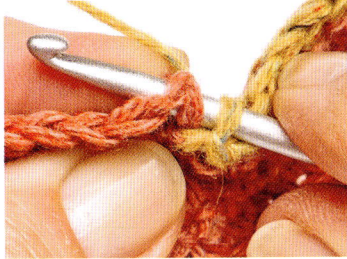

1 Insert the hook into the next stitch in the opposite direction to usual, so that the hook goes under the next chain from back to front.

2 From this position take the hook through the next stitch along from the front to the back so that it has been into two chain stitches and you can see the post of the stitch on the back of the hook. Complete the stitch in the usual way.

BACK POST
In this example the textured stitch has been made in a light coloured yarn, however, for clarity, two yarn shades have been used in the steps.

3 You will notice that the chain that runs along the top of the work is visible on the right side of the work.

4 To work the next stitch, insert the hook into the same place that the second part of the last stitch was worked (so that in effect the chain is used twice) from back to front. From this position take the hook through the next stitch along from the front to the back so that it has been into two chain stitches and you can see the post of the stitch on the back of the hook. Complete the stitch in the usual way.

Jane says

For stitches that have a longer post – such as half treble crochet, treble crochet, or double treble crochet – work as for double crochet but work into the stitch spaces instead of into the chain that runs along the top of the previous row. This means you will be working a little lower than you are used to.

Ribbing

Crochet ribbing is worked in rows rather than in the round.
When used as an edging it is worked in a strip.

BACK LOOP RIBBING

This stitch can be made over any number of stitches.

Make the chain to the required number adding 1 tch.
Foundation row: miss next ch, 1 dc into each ch to end, turn.
Row 1 (RS): 1 ch (does not count as a st), 1 dc into back loop of each st to end, turn.
Repeat row 1 to desired length.

SLIP STITCH RIBBING

This stitch can be made over any number of stitches.

Using a size larger hook, make the chain to the required number adding 1 tch.
Foundation row: miss next ch, 1 ss into each ch to end, turn.
Row 1 (RS): 1 ch (does not count as a st), 1 ss into back loop of each st to end, turn.
Repeat row 1 to desired length.

HALF TREBLE RIBBING

This stitch can be made over any number of stitches.

Make the chain to the required number adding 1 tch.
Foundation row: miss next ch, 1 htr into each ch to end, turn.
Row 1 (RS): 1 ch (does not count as a st), 1 htr into back loop of each st to end, turn.
Repeat row 1 to desired length.

COMBINATION RIBBING

This stitch can be made over any number of stitches.

Using a size larger hook, make the chain to the required number adding 1 tch.
Foundation row: miss next ch, 1ss into each ch to end, turn.

Row 1 (RS): 1ch (does not count as a st), 1 htr into back loop of each st to end, turn.
Row 2 (WS): 1ch (does not count as a st), 1ss into each ch to end, turn.
Repeat as set by row 1 and row 2 to desired length.

Cables

You can create cable designs in crochet by working around the posts of stitches. Cables are made by working into a group of stitches after a set number of missed stitches. The missed stitches are then used to work stitches into. This can be done either by working behind or in front of the stitches you have already made.

CABLE TO THE FRONT

1 Working on a treble crochet background, work to where you want to make the cable.

2 Miss three stitches and work one treble crochet around the front post of each of the next three stitches. You will have created a group of stitches that sits at a slight angle.

3 Working in front of the last three stitches, so that you don't trap the posts, make one treble crochet around the front post of the first missed stitch.

4 Continuing to work in front of the original three stitches, make one treble crochet around the front post of each of the next two missed stitches.

5 You will see that these three stitches sit at an angle in front of the first set of three stitches that were made.

CABLE TO THE BACK

1 Working on a treble crochet background, work to where you want to make the cable.

2 Miss three stitches and work one treble crochet into each of the next three stitches. You will have created a group of stitches that sits at a slight angle.

3 Working behind the last three stitches, so that you don't trap the posts, make one treble crochet around the front post of the first missed stitch. It helps to slightly fold the work forward to see where your stitches need to be made.

4 Continuing to work behind the original three stitches, make one treble crochet around the front post of each of the next two missed stitches.

5 You will see that these three stitches sit at an angle behind the first set of three stitches that were made.

CABLE VARIATIONS
There are lots of ways to use cables in your crochet.

Crossed stitches

Crossed stitches can be made by wrapping the yarn around the hook in an alternative way, or by working the stitches in a different order to usual.

CROSSED DOUBLE CROCHET

This stitch is best worked in the round so that you are constantly working with the right side facing you. The key thing to remember is that you need to take the yarn around the hook in the opposite way to usual before drawing it through the stitch. This can feel strange to begin with.

This stitch can be made over any number of stitches.

Make the chain to the required number adding 1 tch.
Foundation row: miss next ch, insert hook into next ch, take the yarn around the hook in the opposite direction to usual so that it goes under the hook rather than over, catch the yarn and draw through the ch, complete the dc to create a crossed double crochet stitch (cdc).
Continue in this way to end, ss to first ch to join so that you are working in the round.

Row 1: 1 ch (does not count as a st), work a cdc into each stitch to end, ss to join.
Repeat row 1 to desired length.

CROSSED TREBLE CROCHET

It is easier to work this stitch if you make your foundation row over a repeat of an even number of stitches, making a row of double crochet first.

Row 1: 3 ch (counts as 1 tr), miss next st, * 1 tr into next st, from the front insert the hook into the missed st, catch the yarn onto the hook and draw through the st, pull the hook up slightly so that the loop on the hook is not tight, complete the tr in the usual way, miss next st made on previous row; repeat from * to last st, 1 tr into next st.
Repeat row 1 to desired length.

CRISS CROSS STITCH

This is a slight variation to the crossed treble crochet stitch and is best worked in the round. This stitch is a little tricky, but the finish, when working alternate rows, is really effective.

This stitch can be made over any number of stitches.

Make the chain to the required number adding 1 tch.
Work row 1 as for crossed treble crochet stitch.
Row 2: Work as row 1, making the second stitch of the pair of tr sts by working behind the post of the first tr instead of in front.
Repeat as set by row 1 and row 2 to desired length.

Bobbles

Bobbles are a little fiddly to make, especially since they are made with the wrong side of the work facing, which means you need to keep an eye on the stitch count. You also need to move the yarns from back to front to avoid leaving them on the incorrect side of the work.

Bobbles are most effective when worked on a background fabric made using double crochet.

BOBBLE IN SAME YARN SHADE

1 With wrong side facing, work five incomplete treble crochet stitches into the next stitch, leaving one yarn loop on the hook after each stitch so that six loops remain on the hook.

2 Catch the yarn and draw through all yarn loops.

3 Tighten the yarn, but do not pull too tightly since you can lose the stitch at the top of the bobble.

BOBBLE IN CONTRAST YARN SHADE

1 With wrong side facing, crochet to the stitch before the place you want to make a bobble. Work an incomplete treble crochet stitch into the next stitch so that two yarn loops remain on the hook. Bring the yarn to the front.

2 Draw the new yarn shade through the last step of the stitch, leaving a yarn tail of approximately 15cm (6in).

3 Work five incomplete treble crochet stitches into the next stitch, leaving one yarn loop on the hook after each stitch so that six loops remain on the hook.

4 Bring the yarn to the front.

5 Pick up the original (background) yarn and draw through all yarn loops, pulling the yarn across the back of the bobble.

6 Tighten the working yarn but do not pull too tightly since you can lose the stitch at the top of the bobble.

Popcorns

Popcorns are made by working a group of complete stitches into one stitch. These stitches are then joined together by drawing the loop left on the hook by the last stitch through the first.

MAKING A POPCORN AT THE BEGINNING OF A ROW

1 Make three chains (counts as one treble crochet). Make four treble crochet into the same stitch so that you have completed the equivalent of five stitches.

2 Pull the yarn loop on the hook to make it a little larger and remove the hook from the yarn loop, making sure that it does not unravel. Place the hook through the third chain made in Step 1.

3 Place the yarn loop back on the hook. Wrap the yarn round the hook and draw through the loops on the hook to complete the first popcorn.

MAKING A POPCORN MID ROW

1 Place the yarn loop back on the hook.

2 Wrap the yarn around the hook and draw through the loops on the hook to complete.

3 Make five treble crochet stitches into the next stitch.

4 Pull the yarn loop on the hook to make it a little larger, then remove the hook from the yarn loop making sure that it does not unravel.

5 Place the hook through the top of the first stitch of the five double crochet made in Step 1.

Puff stitches

Making a puff stitch is a really easy way to create a textural feature in your work. A puff stitch is worked with the right side of the crochet facing, and it looks best when worked with a background fabric of relatively dense stitches, such as double crochet.

1 Work to where you want to make a puff stitch (they work best mid row).

2 Wrap the yarn around the hook and insert the hook into the next stitch.

3 Use the hook to catch the yarn and draw it through the stitch to the front. Draw the yarn loop up slightly so that the hook is horizontally in line with the top of the last stitch you made. This makes a larger yarn loop on the hook than usual.

4 Repeat Steps 2 and 3, working into the same stitch so that you have a group of yarn loops on the hook. For every step of the stitch you will have two loops on the hook.

5 When you have the required number of yarn loops on the hook, catch the yarn around the hook. With the hook facing downwards, and in a swift movement, draw the yarn through all the loops on the hook to complete the stitch.

Bullion stitches

A bullion stitch is made by wrapping the yarn around the hook, in the same way you would for treble crochet, but with many more yarn loops on the hook. To complete the stitch the yarn is drawn through all the loops to create a stitch that looks like little woodlice.

The stitch can be tricky to work since the yarns can get caught on the hook when drawing the final yarn loop through all the others. Using a hook that has a wider shaft leading up to the handle can help, but you might still find that you end up picking the remaining yarn loops over with your fingers if some of them get caught. Working in this way does not influence the look of the stitch, but it does make it very time-consuming to do.

This bullion stitch takes up the same height as a treble crochet stitch.

When making the first bullion you will need to make three chains to reach the height of the stitch. For subsequent bullion stitches you do not need to make the chain first.

1 Wrap the yarn around the hook eight times, making sure that the yarn loops go up onto the thickest part of the hook's shaft. Guide them onto the hook and hold them in place with your finger if need be.

2 Insert the hook into the next stitch – or ring if working in the round – wrap the yarn around the hook and draw through the stitch or ring so that you have another loop on the hook.

3 Take all the yarn loops up onto the largest part of the shaft of the hook and pinch in place with your fingers.

4 Wrap the yarn around the hook again, making sure that it sits in the crook of the hook as you turn it to catch the yarn.

YARN EFFECTS
Bullions work really well in a slightly hairy or soft yarn, and it is a good idea to use a larger hook than you would usually choose for the yarn.

5 With the hook facing downwards, and with a very quick movement – while still pinching the loops on the hook – draw the final yarn loop through all the loops on the shaft of the hook. Make one chain to complete the stitch.

Decorative stitches

Crochet is incredibly versatile, and you can create lots of lovely pattern combinations using basic stitches and simple techniques. Some stitches create textural work, such as bobbles, popcorns and puff stitches as explained previously, but you can also create decorative chevron and lace designs relatively easily.

I often use clusters in my designs since they can be an easy way to represent a petal on a flower motif, and spike stitches can also be used to create some really lovely effects.

Clusters

A cluster is made by working multiple incomplete stitches into one stitch. The yarn loops from each of these stitches are then grouped into one stitch by drawing the yarn through all the loops on the hook. This example shows a treble crochet cluster over three stitches.

> ### Jane says
>
> You can work clusters over more than three stitches, depending on how bulky you want the cluster to look. Multiples of four and five stitches work well.

1 Insert the hook into the next stitch and work one treble crochet through to the last step of the stitch so that two yarn loops are left on the hook.

2 Repeat this action twice, so that you have a yarn loop left on the hook for each stitch. You will have four loops on the hook.

3 Catch the the yarn and draw through all the yarn loops to complete.

PETALS AND LEAVES
Cluster stitches work well to represent petals or leaves.

SEE ALSO

Filet crochet

The French word *filet* means net, and filet crochet mimics a traditional lacemaking technique where a mesh-like structure is created and some of the spaces are then filled with a style of weaving to create a design that incorporates open and filled-in spaces.

Filet crochet was traditionally worked on a very small hook using fine thread, usually cream or white mercerized cotton.

READING A FILET CHART

It is customary for patterns for filet crochet to be presented in the form of a chart, with minimal written instructions. The charts are made to a square, grid-like format, with each square representing either an 'open' area or a 'closed' group of stitches.

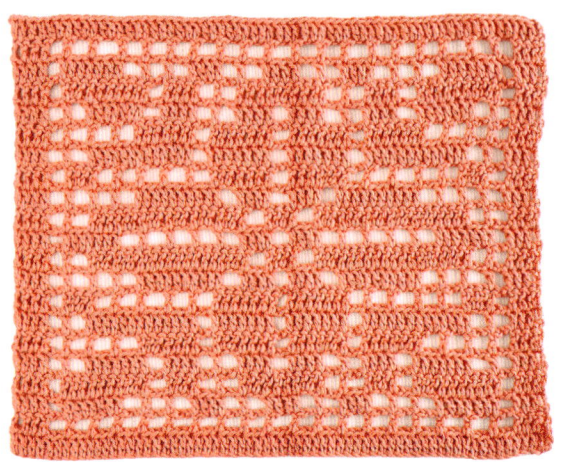

FLOWER FILET CHART

☐ Open square (tr, 2 ch)

▦ Closed square (3 tr)

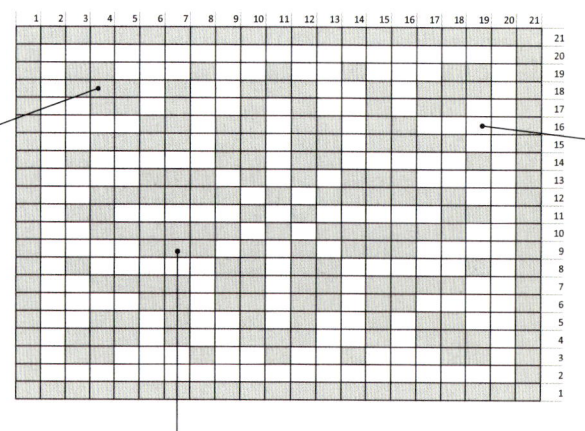

The pattern will tell you what number of stitches a square on the graph represents. It is usual for this to be either three or four stitches.

A shaded square represents a group of stitches and therefore is 'filled in'.

A square with a border that has no shading within it represents a chain space, which is therefore 'open.'

Jane says

Some charts show shaded half squares in the form of vertical rectangles. If the pattern has told you that a square represents four stitches, a half one would be two stitches.

Where shaded squares sit next to each other, they share a common stitch between them. Two shaded squares of three stitches each, for example, would represent a total of five stitches, whereas two shaded squares of four stitches each would represent a total of seven stitches. This is because the blocks on the chart share a common border and so your stitches need to too.

MAKING CHAIN SPACES

Chain spaces are made to create the frame of an open square and link one stitch to another. The chain space is most often made by making one chain, but – as with the number of stitches made to create filled-in blocks – this can change depending on how many open squares need to be represented.

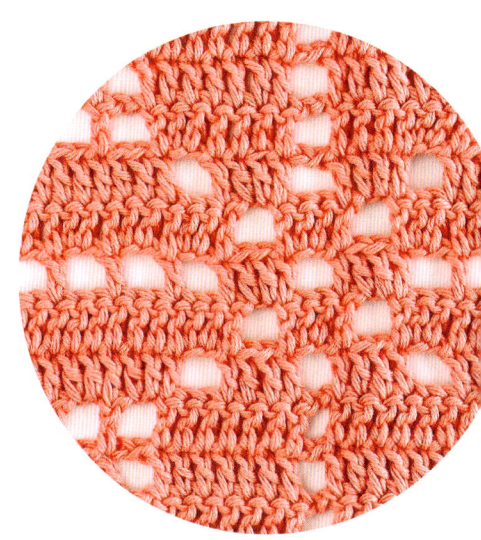

Chain spaces can be made over a large area, or split into smaller parts.

New chain spaces can sit above another chain space.

MAKING FILLED-IN STITCHES

When working into the gap created by the chain you can choose to work either into the chain space (ch-sp) or a specific chain. To fill in a chain space with stitches you need to work into the chains made on the previous row, rather than the space itself.

It is neater to work into the chain rather than the space created by it.

When working in rows you will be making your stitches into the wrong side of the chain, which can be a little fiddly.

Jane says

From time to time a filet chart will include an open square with a 'v' shape at the centre. This could represent two stitches made into the same stitch, or, when made with chain it represents a chain that is slip stitched in place to make an angle, called a lacet.

Chevrons

Chevrons, or zigzags, are made by working a decrease at a specified point in the work and an increase at another. Decreases create a downward point and increases make an upward point.

Chevrons look great when they are worked in lots of colours in a stripe formation. To keep the stitch count correct, the number of stitches that you decrease by needs to be the same as the number of stitches that are increased.

UPWARD AND DOWNWARD POINTS
This sample has been worked dc3tog to create a downward point and 3 dc into the same stitch to create an upward point.

CHAIN SPACES
You can add chain spaces to create more open chevron effects.

Spike stitches

A spike stitch is created by working into rows that are lower than the previous one. It could be that this is one, two or even three rows lower down. Spike stitches are usually made when working double crochet, and are abbreviated to spdc.

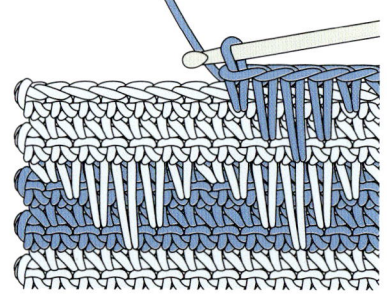

Insert the hook in the stitch indicated on the pattern, and wrap the yarn around the hook. Draw the yarn loop through the stitch and up to the height of the stitches of the working row. Draw the yarn through both loops on the hook to complete the stitch.

SPIKE VARIATIONS
Spike stitches are simple to make and can look especially effective when worked in stripes using a collection of shades.

Beading

Adding beads to crochet is far easier than you might imagine, and creates a striking effect. In most cases the beads are threaded onto your yarn before you start to crochet, although you can also add beads onto the chain at the top of a stitch by using a very fine crochet hook.

One of the tricky aspects of working with beads, at least to begin with, is holding the beads in position so that you don't have to drop the yarn before moving beads to make each beaded stitch. Try holding the beads in small batches over your index finger and bring each bead down the yarn towards the hook with your other index finger as you work.

Even if your chosen yarn is machine washable it is not always a good idea to wash a beaded or sequined fabric in the washing machine. Instead, wash by hand using a mild detergent and be ultra-careful that the beads do not cause threads to snag. Dry flat where possible.

CHOOSING BEADS

Beads are often given a number reference. The number refers to the size of the hole through the centre of the bead rather than the size of the bead itself. The higher the number, the smaller the hole. Size 6/0 beads are suitable for yarns up to DK (3), while size 8/0 beads are suitable for yarns up to 3-ply.

Threading beads

If using lots of beads, thread them onto the yarn in sections, since having too many pre-strung beads can make crochet difficult and affect the tension and appearance of the yarn.

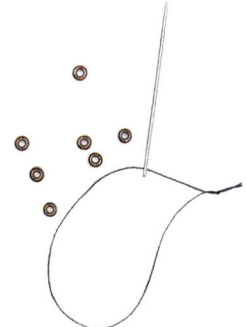

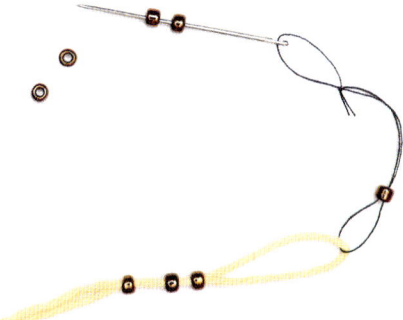

1 Thread a needle with approximately 30cm (12in) of sewing thread and make a small knot to join the ends and form a loop. Move the knot so that it is not in line horizontally with the sewing needle.

2 Place your yarn through the loop created by the sewing thread, leaving a tail end of yarn approximately 10cm (4in) long. Pass the beads over the eye of the needle and push down onto the sewing-thread loop, threading three to five beads at a time. Gently push the beads down onto the double thickness of yarn. Threading the first few beads may be tricky, but it does get easier.

3 It is a good idea to leave one bead at the top of the yarn, close to the sewing-thread loop, each time you thread a few beads. This bead acts as a 'lock' and prevents the yarn from coming out of the thread loop. Once you have threaded all the beads onto the yarn, push them down the yarn and out of the way until they are needed.

SEE ALSO

Crochet Stitches, pages 38–44
The Anatomy of a Stitch, pages 45–47

Jane says

You can add sequins to your crochet when using double crochet. Choose flat sequins, rather than the cupped type, and add them in after the first step of the stitch is completed.

Beaded double crochet (bdc)

Beads are added into the stitch with the wrong side of the work facing.

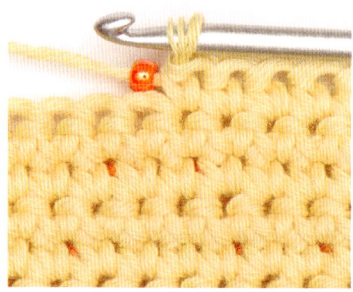

1 With the wrong side facing, work to where the bead is required. Slide the bead along the yarn until it sits as close to the hook as possible.

2 Insert the hook through the stitch and catch the yarn around the hook beyond the bead.

3 Draw the yarn through the stitch, making sure the bead stays in place.

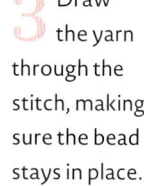

4 Complete the double crochet stitch in the usual way.

Beaded half treble crochet (bhtr)

The advantage of using beaded half treble crochet is that you can place a bead on every row when using turning rows, something you cannot do with beaded double crochet. Note that in the sample shown, the background stitch is double crochet.

PLACING A BEAD TO THE FRONT (BHTR TO FRONT)

These beads are stitched to the front.

1 With the right side facing, work to where the bead is required. Slide the bead along the yarn until it sits as close to the hook as possible.

2 Wrap the yarn around the hook and insert the hook into the stitch.

3 Wrap the yarn around the hook and draw the yarn through the stitch so that there are three loops on the hook.

4 Bring the bead to the facing side by moving it over the yarn on the hook towards you.

5 Wrap the yarn around the hook and complete the stitch by drawing the yarn through all three loops on the hook. Give the yarn a gentle tug to make a tighter stitch than you normally would, which stops the bead wiggling around too much.

Jane says

Using beaded half treble crochet you can add beads to both sides of the work by bringing two beads up the yarn and leaving one at the back and moving one to the front before you complete the stitch. This is a great technique to use for items that will show both sides, such as lacy shawls or scarves.

PLACING A BEAD TO THE BACK (BHTR TO BACK)

1 Work to where the bead is required. Slide the bead along the yarn until it sits as close to the hook as possible.

2 Wrap the yarn around the hook and insert it into the stitch.

These beads are placed to the back of the work.

3 Wrap the yarn around the hook and draw the yarn through the stitch so that there are three loops on hook.

4 Wrap the yarn around the hook and complete the stitch by drawing the yarn through all three loops on the hook.

5 Give the yarn a gentle tug to make a tighter stitch than you normally would, which stops the bead wiggling around too much.

Beaded treble crochet (btr)

When working beaded treble crochet in the round you can place beads on every stitch and every round. When working in rows you can place beads on alternate rows. Beads are added into the stitch with the wrong side of the work facing.

1 With the wrong side facing, work to where a bead is required and wrap the yarn around the hook.

2 Insert the hook into the next stitch. Draw the yarn through the stitch so that there are three loops on the hook.

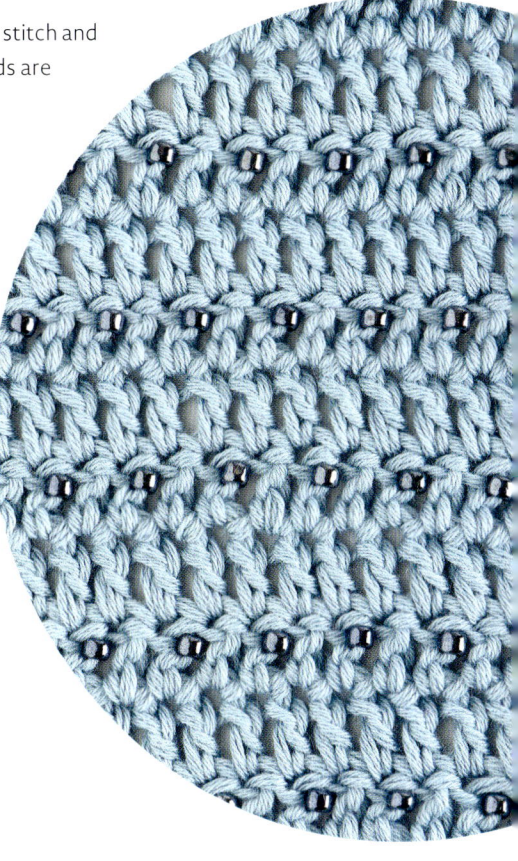

3 Wrap the yarn around the hook and draw it through two loops so that there are two loops left on the hook.

4 Slide the bead as far as you can towards the crochet hook.

5 Catch the yarn beyond the bead and pull through two loops to complete the stitch.

Jane says

You can add more than one bead to the post of the stitch when making beaded double trebles. This can look particularly effective when making fan patterns. To make a beaded double treble, thread two beads onto the yarn for every stitch you want to place beads on, and catch them into the working stitch on the final two steps of making.

Beaded edgings

Many beaded edgings work best if you create them on the final row of your crochet rather than on the first, because the beads will sit flat and neat.

THREE-BEAD EDGING
To make a three-bead edging, allow three beads per stitch and thread them onto the yarn before you start to crochet.

2 Insert the hook into the next stitch and catch the yarn with the hook beyond the group of three beads. Draw the yarn through the stitch and complete the double crochet in the usual way.

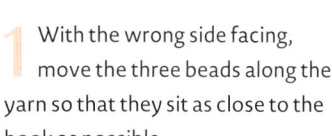

1 With the wrong side facing, move the three beads along the yarn so that they sit as close to the hook as possible.

BEADED LOOPS
You can choose to create beaded loops that are all the same size, or you could make them all to a slightly different length, dependent on how many beads you choose to add to the yarn for each one. This sample shows a mix of beaded loop lengths.

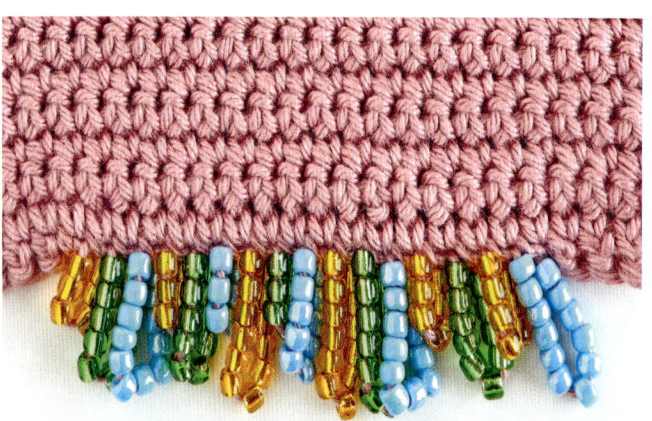

With wrong side facing, work as for Three-Bead Edging, moving your chosen number of beads up to the top of the yarn before catching the yarn beyond the beads and drawing through the stitch.

BEADED LOOPS BETWEEN ROWS

Allowing six beads for every alternate stitch, thread the beads onto the yarn before you start to crochet. You will need to work this design over an odd number of stitches, and beads are placed with the wrong side of the work facing as follows:

Row 1 (WS): 1 ch, (does not count as a st), 1 dc into st at base of 1 ch, * working as for beaded loops make a beaded loop with 6 beads on it into next st, 1 dc into next st; repeat from * to end, turn.
Row 2 (RS): 3 ch, (count as 1 dc), [making sure that 3 beads sit either side of the hook 1 dc into next beaded loop, 1 ch] to last st, 1 dc into next st, turn.
Row 3 (WS): 1 ch, (does not count as a st), 1 dc into st at base of 1-ch, * 1 dc into next st, 1 dc into next ch-sp] to last 2 sts, 1 dc into next st, 1 dc into 3rd ch of tch, fasten off.

BEADED CHAIN EDGE

Worked over a multiple of 6 sts + 1 st, thread eight beads onto the yarn for each beaded loop.

(WS): 1 ch (does not count as a st), 1 dc into st at base of 1 ch, 1 bdc into next st, make 7 beaded chain by moving a bead up the yarn to sit close to the hook and catching the yarn beyond the bead to make a chain for each one, miss 4 sts, 1 dc into next st, 1 bdc into next st; repeat from * to end.

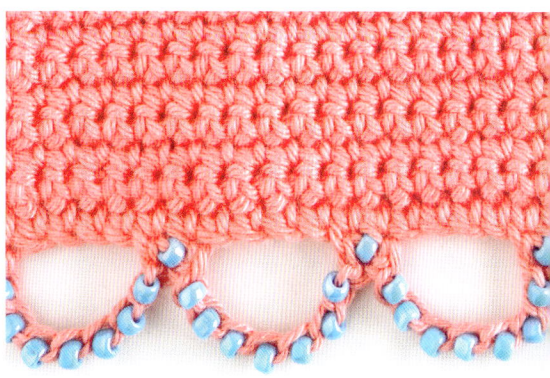

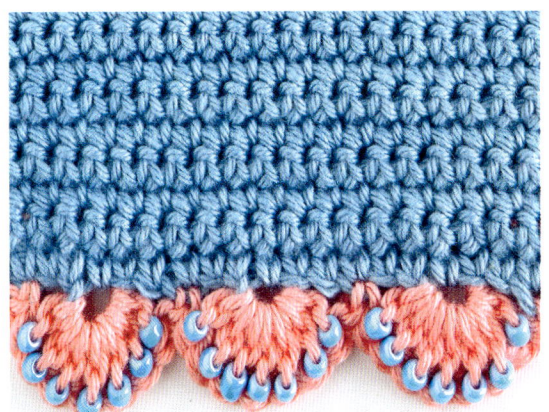

BEADED FANS

Worked over a multiple of 6 sts + 1 st, thread seven beads onto the yarn for each fan.

(WS): 1 ch (does not count as a st), 1 dc into st at base of 1 ch, * miss next 2 sts, 7 btr into next st, miss 2 sts, 1 dc into next st; repeat from * to end.

Colour work

The three main techniques for creating multicoloured crochet fabrics are intarsia, tapestry and mosaic crochet. Each method is worked in a different way and creates a fabric with its own unique characteristics.

Colour theory

The origin of colour theory dates back hundreds of years, with English physicist Sir Isaac Newton credited as the pioneer of experiments with sunlight and prisms. The outcome of Newton's experiments created the basis of colour theory and the recognition of three definitive primary colours that, when mixed in pairs create three further colours, referred to as secondary colours, along with a seventh colour that is a combination of all shades mixed together.

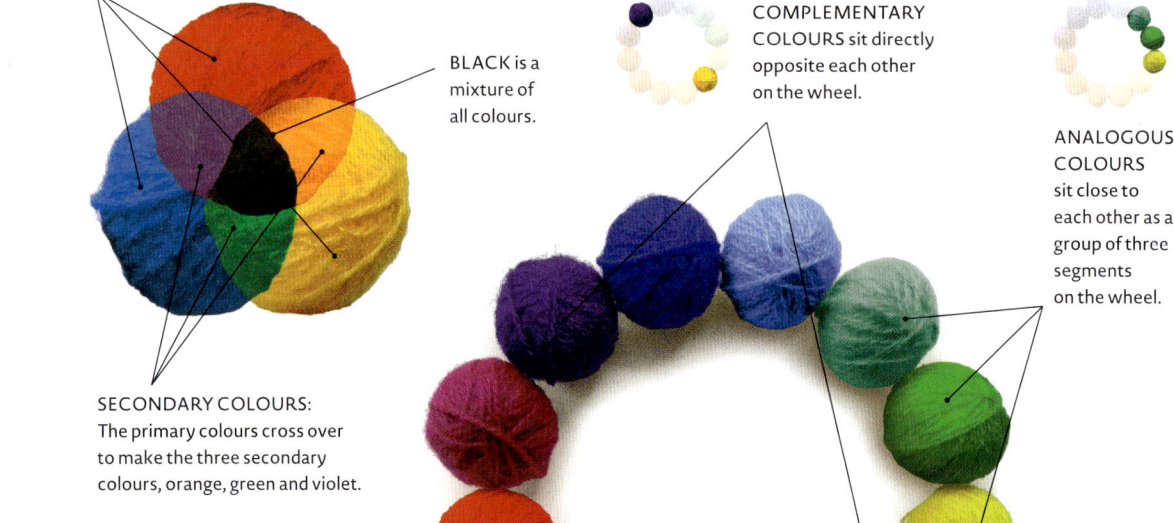

THE THREE PRIMARY COLOURS are red, yellow and blue.

BLACK is a mixture of all colours.

SECONDARY COLOURS: The primary colours cross over to make the three secondary colours, orange, green and violet.

COMPLEMENTARY COLOURS sit directly opposite each other on the wheel.

ANALOGOUS COLOURS sit close to each other as a group of three segments on the wheel.

MONOCHROMATIC COLOURS sit in a range within a single segment of the colour wheel. Each colour within the group has different depths of the same shade.

TRIADIC COLOURS are three groups of colours that sit evenly spaced on the wheel.

SEE ALSO

Sir Isaac Newton created the first colour wheel in 1666, which showed how all colours are derived from the three primary colours. Since then, artists and scientists have developed it further to create groupings of colour that help us make decisions about which colours go together.

Jane says

I am very fortunate to be able to pick my palettes from a large selection of yarns. I often mix yarns from various ranges to achieve the exact colour combination of shades that I want, using research and mood boards as inspiration. I don't believe that there are any colours that don't go together, but you do need to consider the proportions that different shades are used in, since the relationship between colours and the amounts used influences the appearance of each of them.

When I build a palette I tend to pick a few colours that work together monochromatically first. Then I choose a dark shade and a light one to sit at opposite ends of this spectrum. I also like to add in a couple of shades from the complementary group of colours that will provide a pop of colour.

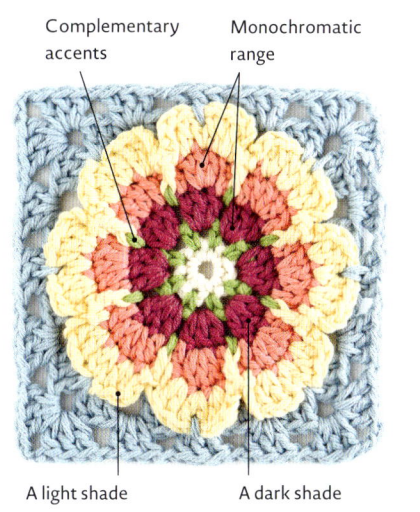

Complementary accents

Monochromatic range

A light shade

A dark shade

Working from a chart

Whether working a crochet design using the intarsia, tapestry or mosaic techniques, the project pattern will usually provide you with a chart, which cuts down on written instructions and gives a visual representation of how the finished fabric will look.

If the chart is in graph form, each square represents a stitch. On some charts the squares are coloured to indicate which shade of yarn to use, while on charts that are not printed in colour the squares may contain a symbol that is referred to in a key.

INTARSIA CROCHET CHART

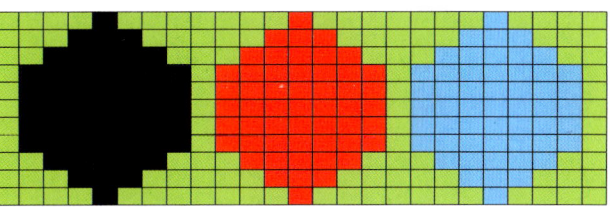

If the chart features large areas of a single colour, with more than two or three colours in the design, and large gaps of stitches between shade changes, then it is probably an intarsia chart.

TAPESTRY CROCHET CHART

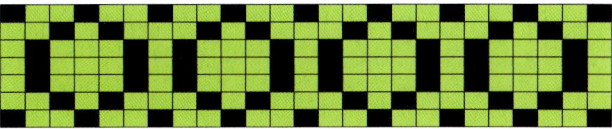

If the chart features just a couple of yarn shades repeated across a row, then the chances are it is a chart for tapestry crochet. On this kind of chart the number of stitches in each section of alternate colours is likely to be no more than about seven. Tapestry charts usually comprise stripes of repeated geometric-style designs. Tapestry crochet charts can look very similar to those for mosaic crochet so make sure you look at the pattern instructions closely before starting work.

MOSAIC CROCHET CHART

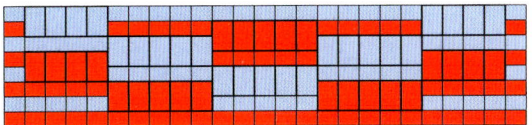

Mosaic crochet designs are often charted with each square representing a stitch. Single squares on a row represent a double crochet stitch in a particular colour. A vertical line of three squares in the same shade represents a treble crochet stitch.

Intarsia crochet

The word intarsia was first used in the fifteenth century in reference to an intricate style of marquetry. In intarsia knitting, each yarn shade creates a separate area of fabric with no yarns carried across the back of the work from one position to another.

A crochet design worked using the intarsia technique can only be created when working turned rows, rather than in the round.

To work intarsia crochet you need to prepare your yarn before you start. You can make small balls, use ready-made yarn bobbins or wind butterfly bobbins.

BUTTERFLY BOBBIN

A butterfly yarn bobbin is made by wrapping the yarn around your fingers and is a good alternative to using a plastic, ready-made bobbin. It is perfect for smaller areas of colour, but be careful not to make it too big since yarn can become tangled.

If you know how many stitches the yarn needs to make, you can work out how much yarn to wind onto the bobbin by doing a quick test. Using the stitch that the pattern is written for (intarsia crochet is often worked in double crochet), crochet ten stitches, unravel, and measure the amount of yarn used to make the stitches. Allowing a little extra for yarn tails and movement between rows, multiply this amount by the number of stitches you need to make.

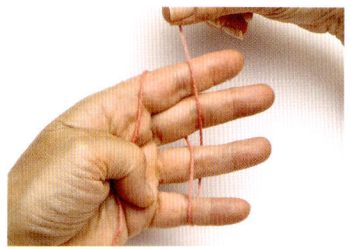

1 Secure the tail end of yarn at the crook of your thumb.

2 Wrap the yarn around your fingers in a figure eight, keeping the yarn tail in place.

3 When you have the required amount of yarn wrapped around your fingers, let the yarn tail drop and gently remove the yarn from your fingers.

4 Wrap the yarn end that links to the main ball around the centre of the figure eight.

5 Cut the yarn end and secure by threading it under the wound yarn.

6 To use the bobbin, gently pull the original yarn tail (that sat in the crook of your thumb) to release the yarn as required.

CHANGING YARN SHADE RIGHT SIDE

As a rule, the first row of a chart will be right-side facing. A right-side row of the chart is read from right to left and a wrong-side row is read from left to right – vice versa if you are left-handed.

Once you have completed your stitches using your first yarn shade and want to change colour, do so on the final step of the stitch made before the colour change. The example shown is with double crochet, and the method is exactly the same for treble crochet.

BAD COLOUR CHANGE
When the yarn is not changed on the final step of the stitch you can see the yarn showing through the stitches either side of the join.

GOOD COLOUR CHANGE
When the yarn is changed on the final step of the stitch, the crossover point has a neater appearance.

1 When working on the right side, complete the first step of the last stitch before the colour change so that two yarn loops remain on the hook.

2 Keeping the yarn tail at the back of the work, draw the new yarn shade through the remaining loops on the hook to complete the stitch.

3 The yarn loop left on the hook will be the new shade of yarn. This will ensure that the chain that runs along the top of the next stitch is the correct shade.

CHANGING YARN SHADE WRONG SIDE

You may find that the first row where you need to add in a new yarn shade is wrong-side facing, in which case you need to bring the yarn forward. The example shown is of double crochet, and the method is exactly the same for treble crochet.

1 When working on the wrong side, complete the first step of the last stitch before the colour change so that two yarn loops remain on the hook. Bring the yarn forward.

2 Keeping the yarn tail at the front of the work, draw the new yarn shade through the remaining loops on the hook to complete the stitch.

3 The yarn loop left on the hook will be the new shade of yarn. This will ensure that the chain that runs along the top of the next stitch is the correct shade.

WORKING SUBSEQUENT ROWS

Whether your yarns run from a small ball or a bobbin, they are left in place and dangle from the work. When you work the next row of crochet the yarn will be ready for you to use in the position that you left it.

When working a right-side row the yarns will be on the reverse side of the work. Change yarn shade on the final step of the stitch before the colour change.

When working a wrong-side row the yarns will be on the side of the work facing you. When the first step of the final stitch in the first shade is complete, bring the yarn forward. Pick up the new shade so that you are holding it behind the work. Complete the stitch to change yarn shade on the final step of the stitch before the colour change.

Tapestry crochet

This technique is comparable to Fair Isle knitting. Yarn shades are carried from one point in the work to another to create a double thickness fabric made up of stitches and stranded yarns across the reverse side. Tapestry crochet is usually worked using two shades of yarn per row, which creates a nice pattern, but also a double-thickness fabric for extra warmth.

To change yarn shade, work as for intarsia, but instead of leaving the finished-with dangling, it will be used again in the same row. To carry the yarn to where you need it, use the stranding or weaving techniques.

STRANDING

Use the stranding technique when the gap between colours is not more than three stitches. If you are working with the wrong side of the work facing you, it is important to remember not to leave your yarns on the side of the work facing away from you.

Draw the yarn not in use across the back of the made stitches and use it to complete the final stitch in order to change colour. When the yarn travels across the work, make sure you do not overpull it, and try to keep a consistent tension.

WEAVING IN

Use the weaving-in method when the gap between colours is four or more stitches.

This method is similar to stranding but, to avoid a large float of yarn across the reverse of the work, you crochet over the top of the yarn strand to catch it into the stitch every few stitches.

Hold the yarn horizontally in line with the top of the previous row. Insert the hook into the next stitch and complete the stitch so that you trap the yarn strand within it.

Mosaic crochet

Mosaic crochet uses just one colour of yarn per row, but it has the appearance of a fabric that has used two. Mosaic designs are often geometric (like tapestry) but can also be used to create picture-style fabrics like intarsia. Mosaic crochet is worked using a combination of double and treble crochet stitches and, unlike intarsia and tapestry, each row of crochet is made using just one colour, with rows alternating the shades so that there is no need to change yarn shade mid row.

Mosaic crochet is often only worked with the right-side facing in rows, which means that the yarn needs to be fastened off and cut at the end of a row and joined in at the beginning of a row. The technique uses quite a lot of yarn and makes a thick, ruglike fabric.

FOUNDATION ROWS

Mosaic pattern repeats often start once a couple of foundation rows have been worked. The chain and first foundation row are usually made in a single shade that is fastened off at the end of the row. Do not turn the work and join the second shade into the back loop of the first stitch at the beginning of the row. Work another row of crochet into the back loop of all stitches and fasten off at the end of the row.

INTERLOCKED AND OVERLAY STITCHES

Once the first two foundation rows have been worked, use a combination of interlocked and overlay stitches to create the fabric.

Make interlocked stitches by working double crochet into the back loop of the stitches on the previous row.

Make overlay stitches by working double crochet into the remaining front loop of the chain left behind on the stitches two rows down. Work in front of the previous row so that two double layers of fabric are created.

INSET STITCHES

To work in turned rows so that you can create a design using right-side and wrong-side stitches, you can use chain lengths between stitches to replace double crochet stitches worked into the back loop. Chains use less yarn than double crochet, but be careful of the tension since chains can be a little tighter.

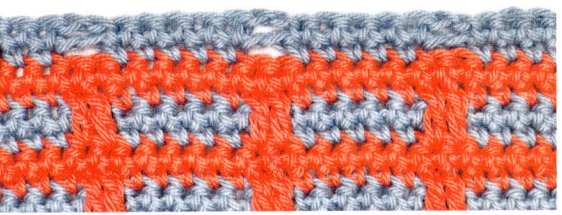

Here the stitches have been missed and replaced with chain over two rows.

Here the missed stitches are being worked into on the next row.

Borders, edgings and embellishments

THE CRAFT OF CROCHET IS SO VERSATILE THAT IT
LENDS ITSELF BEAUTIFULLY TO THE CREATION OF
BORDERS, EDGINGS AND EMBELLISHMENTS, WHICH
CAN ALL BE ADDED TO PRODUCE A STUNNING
FINISHING TOUCH.

Borders and edgings

Crocheted borders and edgings give crochet fabrics a professional-looking finish: think of them in terms of a perfect frame around a work of art.

There will be times when you need to do some mathematical thinking to make sure pattern repeats fit the edges you want to add them to, but one of the great things about crochet is that you can play around with stitch counts by either adding a few stitches or taking some away to make things work.

To make a border or edging directly onto a crochet fabric, you will need to pick up stitches along the side edges. You can do this a row or two before you make the decorative stitches, or at the same time.

Picking up stitches along the bottom edge

To add an edging to the bottom of your crochet fabric you need to crochet into the remaining part of the foundation chain. Depending on how you made your foundation row into the chain, you will either have one yarn loop left on the edge or two.

Hold the piece with the foundation edge facing upwards and insert the hook into the first chain of the foundation chain. Work the turning chain into this place. If working double crochet, make the first stitch into the chain at the base of the turning chain. If working a stitch with a longer post the turning chain will count as your first stitch. Make your next stitches into the remaining side of the foundation chains.

Picking up stitches along the top edge

To add a border or edging to the top of your crochet fabric, work as if adding another row of crochet, joining in your new yarn as on page 64.

SEE ALSO
Common Pattern Abbreviations, page 138
Crochet Stitches, pages 38–44
Joining In a New Yarn, pages 63–66
Sewn Embellishments, pages 112–114

Picking up stitches along a side edge: double crochet

The composition of a double crochet stitch is slightly wider than it is tall, so if you want to pick up stitches along a side edge of a double crochet fabric you will mostly pick up one stitch for each row of crochet.

Work your edging stitches into the stitch space between the first and second stitch of the row: this space is quite clear when looking at a wrong-side row, but a little tighter on a right-side row.

So that the edging doesn't end up with too many stitches, miss a stitch space every now and then (see Jane Says, below).

Picking up stitches along a side edge: treble crochet

Since treble crochet is worked with turning chains that count as stitches at the edges, it is not as easy to pick up stitches as when working into double crochet. If you pick up into the stitch spaces you will accentuate the gap between stitches and create a hole, so work directly into the post of the edge stitches instead. This means you will work into a turning chain or into a true stitch. You may need to use a slightly sharper hook to do this.

Jane says

If you have created a crochet fabric from a combination of stitches, it is a good idea to work some calculations before you start picking up the stitches. Measure the edge of the fabric and note how many stitches you need to pick up. Divide the number of stitches by the measurement in centimetres, which will give you the number of stitches you need to pick up within that centimetre measurement. You may find it helpful to put pins in at centimetre intervals.

Turning corners

To add an edging around a shape with definite corners, you need to increase the stitch count so that the border lies flat and does not 'cup' at the corner edge.

When working double crochet it is usual to make three stitches into the corner stitch. When working treble crochet you will probably need to make five stitches into the corner stitch. If working an edging or border made of a few rows, you may need to increase on more than one row.

If working right-side rows you may need to move the corner stitch over by one stitch to make sure you create an unbiased corner. If you are right-handed, move the stitch one place to the right. If you are left-handed, move it one place to the left. When working a deep border over lots of rows you may need to do this more than once.

Picot edging

To make an edging using picots, it is a good idea to spread them out a little and work them every three, four or five stitches.

To make a single picot, start by making 1 dc, 3 ch, ss into the st at base of 3 ch by working into the front loop of the ch at the top of the dc at the base of 3 ch and into the left side of the post of the same st at the same time.

Crown picot (CP)

1 Start by making 1 dc, 3 ch, ss into the st at base of 3-ch by working into the front loop of the ch at the top of the dc at the base of 3 ch and into the left side of the post of the same st at the same time so that the hook goes under 2 yarn loops. (First picot made.)

2 3 ch, ss into the remaining side of the ss made at the base of the first picot, the front loop of the ch at the top of the dc at the base of same picot and into the left side of the post of the same st at the same time so that the hook goes under 3 yarn loops. (Second picot made.)

3 3 ch, ss into the remaining side of the ss made at the base of the second picot, the remaining side of the ss made at the base of the first picot, the front loop of the ch at the top of the dc at the base of first picot, and into the left side of the post of the same st at the same time so that the hook is under 3 yarn loops. (Third picot made.)

4 1 dc into same st at base of the crown picot to complete.

Shell edging

A shell edge is created by working a group of stitches with long posts into the same stitch. Shells are usually made using an odd number of stitches such as five or seven.

Worked over multiples of 6 + 1
Start by making 1 dc, [miss 2 sts, 7 tr into next st, miss 2 sts, 1 dc into next st] to end.

Fan edging

A fan edge is worked in much the same way as a shell edge, but chains are added between the stitches.

Worked over multiples of 6 + 1
Start by making 1 dc, * 1 ch, miss 2 sts, 1 tr into next st, [1 ch, 1 tr into same st] four times, miss 2 sts, 1 dc into next st; repeat from * to end.

Ruffles

To make a ruffle edge you simply need to increase the stitch count. The more stitches you make the more ruffled the edge will be. The edging will be very wavy, so use your fingers to neaten the concertina effect.

Ruffles can be made over any number of stitches. Join the yarn into the first st by making 1 ch + 2 ch (counts as 1 tr), 4 tr into st at base of 3-ch, 5 tr into each st to end, fasten off.

Cheat's crab stitch

Crab stitch is also known as reverse double crochet. It makes an unusual 'bound' edging, but can be a difficult stitch to create neatly, especially since it is worked in an opposite direction to the usual way. Making this cheat's version is much easier and the results are incredibly similar.

1 At the beginning of the row, join the yarn by working one chain (does not count as a stitch). Insert the hook into the stitch at the base of the chain and draw the yarn through the stitch so that two yarn loops are on the hook. It is a good idea to draw the yarn through a little looser than you usually would.

2 Rotate the hook in an anticlockwise direction so that you twist the yarn loops on the hook.

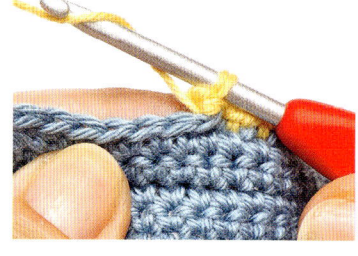

CRAB STITCH
A traditional crab stitch is worked from left to right.

3 Wrap the yarn around the hook.

CHEAT'S CRAB STITCH
Because the row is worked from right to left instead of left to right, the angled direction of the stitch is a mirror-image to that of the traditional crab stitch.

4 Complete the stitch by drawing the yarn through the two loops on the hook. Insert the hook into the next stitch and repeat.

Surface crochet

Surface crochet is a form of embellishment worked into the right side of the finished crochet fabric. It looks like chain stitch.

1 Hold the yarn at the reverse side of the work. From the front, insert the hook into the desired stitch space.

2 Catch the yarn around the hook on the reverse side of the work.

3 Draw the yarn through to the front of the work, making sure to anchor the tail end of yarn at the back of the work so that the stitches do not slip through to the front (two loops on the hook).

4 Draw the last loop made through the first one on the hook to create a slip stitch. You will see that crochet stitches make consistent holes, so simply choose which direction you want your stitches to follow and insert the hook into the next position and repeat Steps 2–3 to complete the effect.

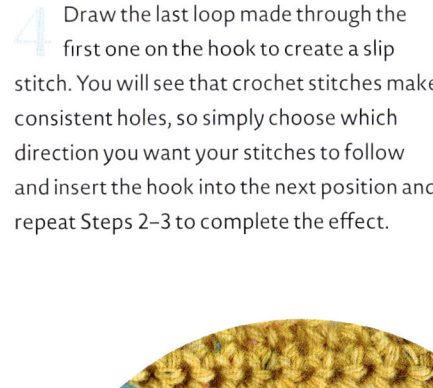

5 To fasten off, cut the yarn tail and draw through to the front of the work. This can be done midway through the crochet fabric or at an edge, as here.

Sewn embellishments

A fabric made from double crochet creates the perfect base for sewn embellishments, since it features consistent holes between stitches and rows, much like Aida. The examples here are worked onto a double crochet fabric, with some of them worked into stitch spaces and others worked by splitting through the yarns.

For all techniques, you will need a sewing needle with an eye large enough to take your chosen yarn. A good length to work with is 50cm (20in), with a knot in the tail end.

Unless otherwise specified, start by inserting the needle through a stitch space in the fabric, from back to front.

Jane says

Adding sewn stitches to a crochet fabric can create some lovely effects. I often use French knots to add detail to the centre of crochet flowers, and basic running stitch can echo the lovely Indian technique of Kantha stitching. Backstitch is a strong stitch to use to join crochet pieces together, but can also be used to add a decorative effect.

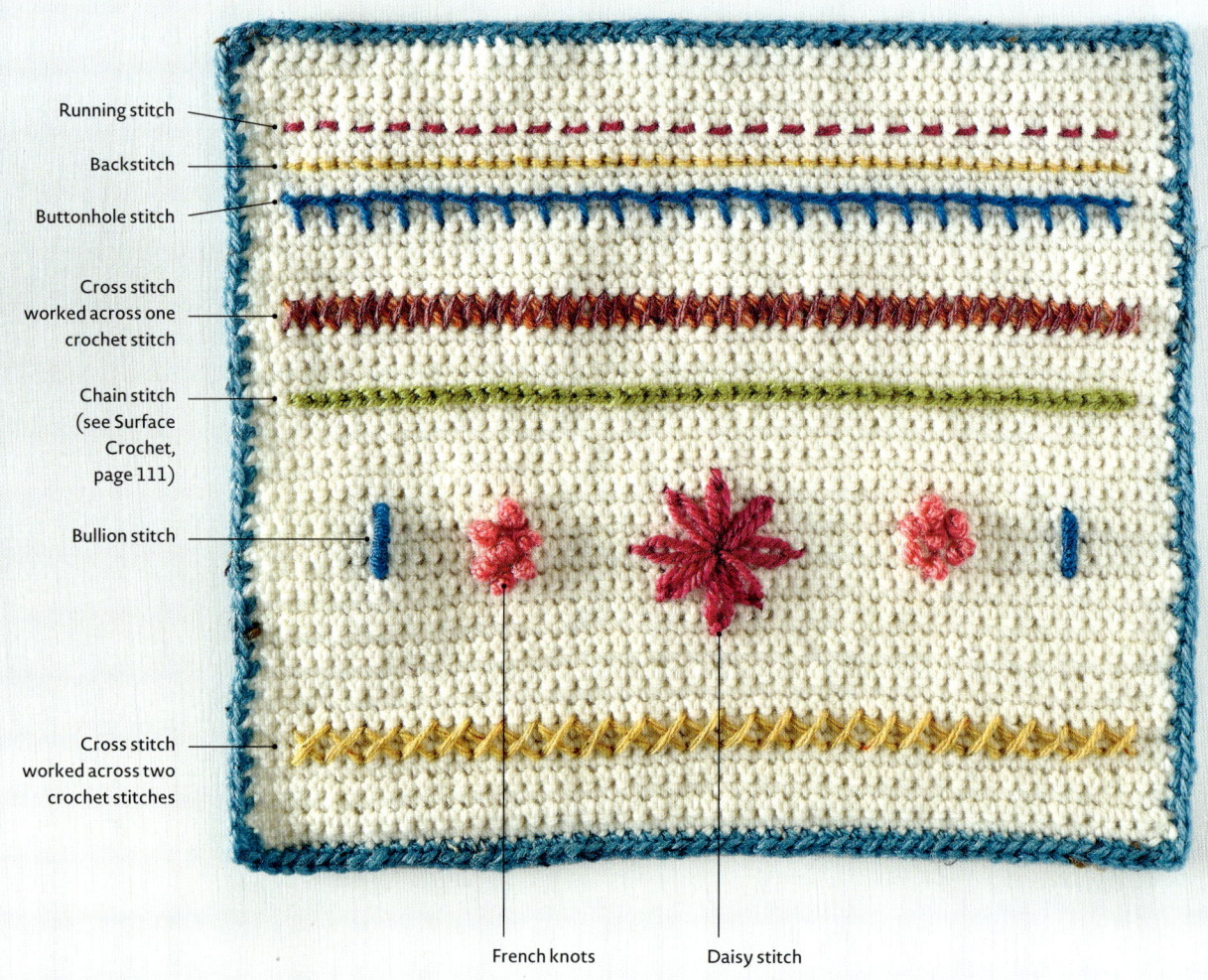

Running stitch

Backstitch

Buttonhole stitch

Cross stitch worked across one crochet stitch

Chain stitch (see Surface Crochet, page 111)

Bullion stitch

Cross stitch worked across two crochet stitches

French knots   Daisy stitch

Running stitch

This is probably the most basic sewn stitch. It is easy to create but it can be really effective. In the example shown, the stitches are worked over one stitch at a time. You can choose to work over more – maybe two or three stitches at a time – but be sure to keep the stitch size consistent.

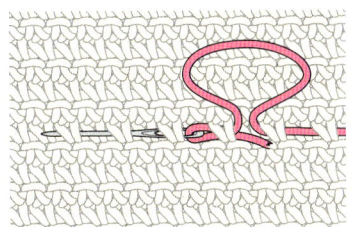

Working along the same row of crochet, insert the needle into the next stitch space along from the front, and draw the yarn through to the reverse side. Continue working in the same way to complete the required number of stitches.

Cross stitch

This stitch is worked over two rows of double crochet using the spaces between each stitch to draw the sewing needle through. As the name suggests, one stitch crosses over another to create an X shape.

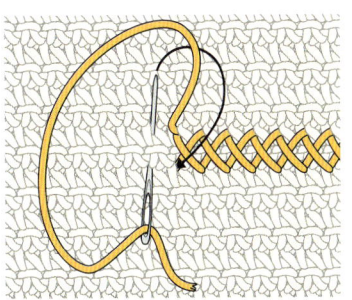

Working along the stitch spaces made a row below, insert the needle from the front into the next stitch space diagonally along, and bring the needle through the space that sits directly above. Draw the yarn through to the right side. Working along the stitch spaces two rows below, insert the needle from the front into the space diagonally to the right (almost like you are working back on yourself) and draw the yarn through to the reverse side.

Backstitch

To make backstitch you will be working forward by the space of a stitch, then back over that space.

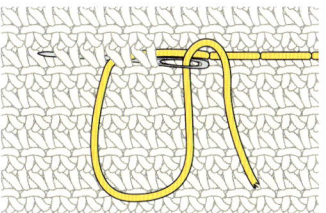

Make one running stitch bringing the needle to the front of the fabric once the stitch is complete. Take the needle back on itself and insert it into the place where the last stitch ends, without splitting through the stitch. Bring the needle forward to the front of the work one more stitch along and repeat.

Daisy stitch

Before you start to make the daisy, decide on a central point and how many petals you want to create.

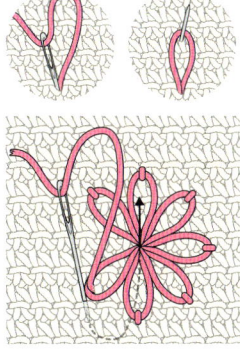

Working each chain from the centre point outward, secure each 'petal' in place by making a smaller stitch at the top of it, much like a running stitch, instead of another chain stitch.

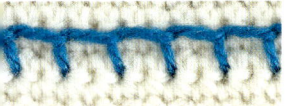

Buttonhole stitch

This stitch is traditionally used to finish the edge of afghans to prevent fraying and wear. It can also be used to secure folded hems and to edge a buttonhole. You can work this stitch from right to left or left to right.

Before you start, decide how far into the crochet fabric you want to make the stitches. This might be one row of crochet or a couple of stitches in from the edge of the fabric. Make sure your stitches are even and consistent.

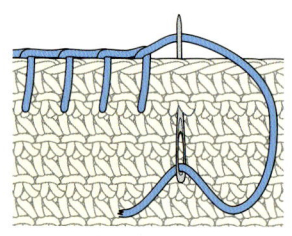

To make the first stitch, take the thread around the edge of the work and insert the needle through the same stitch from back to front. Holding the needle horizontally in line with the edge of the crochet fabric, insert it through the stitch you have just made so that the needle sits at the very edge of the work. Take the needle vertically up towards the edge of the fabric and wrap the yarn around the reverse of it.

French knot

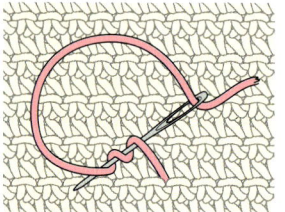

Also known as a French dot, knotted stitch or twisted knot stitch, this stitch is used to create a small, three-dimensional knot on the front of the work. Often used at the centre of flowers in embroideries, this stitch can also be used on toys to create facial features and embellishments. Unlike the other sewn stitches, you need to work so that you split through the yarn used to make the crochet fabric, rather than stitching into stitch spaces.

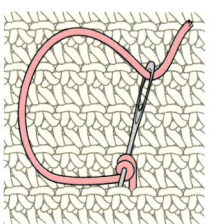

Holding the needle close to the crochet and working relatively tightly, wrap the yarn around the needle twice. From the front, insert the needle through the work very close to where the yarn has already come through. Draw the needle through to the back of the work to create a knot.

Bullion stitch

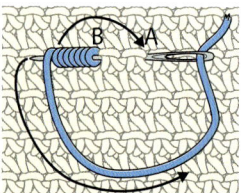

Also known as a bullion knot, coil stitch, grub knot, post stitch, worm stitch or Porto Rico rose, this decorative stitch is worked by wrapping the yarn around the sewing needle before inserting it through the fabric. It is a good idea to use a sewing needle that does not go too wide at the eye end, so that the wrapped yarn is consistently the same size. As for the French knot, you need to work so that you split through the yarn used to make the crochet fabric rather than stitching into stitch spaces.

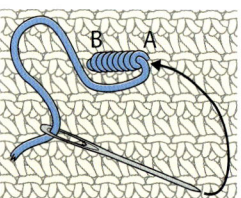

Make the equivalent of a backstitch, but do not tighten the yarn. Bring the needle through the work from the back to the front at the point where the stitch started. Do not pull the needle all the way through the work. Wrap the yarn around the needle so that it lines up on the shaft. Do not cross the yarn over itself when you do this. The more times you wrap the yarn, the longer the stitch will be. Carefully draw the needle through the yarn wraps. Insert the needle through from the front to back at the other end of the stitch to complete.

Buttons and buttonholes

It is not always easy to find buttons that complement your project perfectly, so you can make your own. Creating the right buttonhole to match your button will also help you achieve a professional look.

Horizontal buttonhole

The easiest buttonhole to make is a horizontal one worked over a couple of rows. Before you start to crochet, work out how many stitches you need to miss and how many chains you need to make to fit your selected button. This buttonhole is best worked over double crochet.

(WS): Crochet to where you want to make the buttonhole. Make your chain loop, miss the required number of stitches, continue to crochet to the end of the row.
(RS): On the next row, fill the chain loop up with double crochet stitches to your required stitch count.

HORIZONTAL BUTTONHOLE MID ROW   HORIZONTAL BUTTONHOLE ON EDGE

Vertical buttonhole

This vertical buttonhole is stitched in treble crochet and worked over two rows by making a length of chain between two stitches on one row and working into it on the next one.

Row 1 (WS): 3 ch (counts as 1 tr), * 1 tr into each st to the point where you want to make a buttonhole, 6 ch, 1 tr into next st, 1 tr into each st to next buttonhole; repeat from * to end, turn.

Row 2 (RS): 3 ch (counts as 1 tr), * 1 tr into each st to ch-sp, miss next st at base of ch, ss into next ch-sp, miss next st at base of ch, 1 tr into each st to next buttonhole; repeat from * to end, turn.
Row 3 (WS): 3 ch (counts as 1 tr), * 1 tr into each st to ss made at top of next ch-sp, 2 tr into ss, 1 tr into each st to next buttonhole; repeat from * to end, turn.

SEE ALSO

Bobbles, page 82
Common Pattern Abbreviations, page 138
Crochet Stitches, pages 38–44

Stuffed bobble button

You can make small buttons by filling a bobble stitch with a little bit of toy stuffing or a wooden bead. Using the instructions on page 82, make a bobble to the point where all the yarn loops remain on the hook. Then pop the stuffing or bead into the bobble before you draw the yarn through all yarn loops to complete the stitch.

Covering a button

For this technique you will need a button with a shank, rather than holes drilled through the centre, with a diameter of approximately 2.5cm (1in).

Make a magic loop (see page 61).
Foundation round: 3 ch (counts as 1 tr), fill the magic loop with tr stitches (the example shows a total of 15 sts including the tch), ss to join, tighten magic loop.
Round 1: 1 ch (does not count as a st), 1 tr into back loop of st at base of 1-ch, 1 tr into back loop of all sts to end, ss to join, fasten off leaving a tail end of yarn approximately 20cm (8in) long.
Sew in the yarn tail that made the magic loop.

Thread a needle with the yarn tail and oversew around all the stitches. Insert the button (shank side up) and pull the yarn tail to tighten the crochet around the button. Sew the yarn in and cut the remaining tail.

Dorset button

You can create an effective decorative button using a small ring to make a Dorset button. This type of button originates from the Dorset area in England, where a slice of goat or sheep horn was traditionally used. These days you can source plastic or metal rings instead.

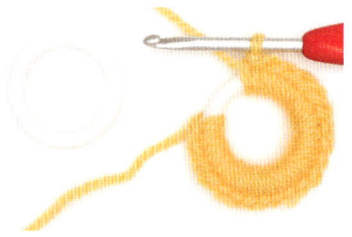

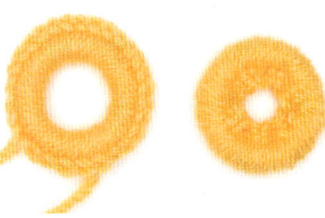

1 Work double crochet or buttonhole stitch (see page 114) around the circumference of the ring, making sure the stitches are tightly packed so you can't see the internal ring between them.

2 Turn the chain that runs along the outside edge of the ring to the centre.

3 If using more than one shade of yarn, fasten off at this point; otherwise measure off a length of yarn, thread through a tapestry needle, and draw through the final chain. If using an alternative shade, thread a tapestry needle with a length of yarn and knot the tail end of yarn.

4 Create spokes by wrapping the yarn around the ring. Think of this in terms of a clock face and wrap 12 o'clock to 6 o'clock, 3 o'clock to 9 o'clock, then add spokes in between these.

5 If using more than one shade of yarn, fasten off at this point; otherwise measure off a length of yarn, thread through a tapestry needle, and draw through the final chain. If using an alternative shade, thread a tapestry needle with a length of yarn and knot the tail end of yarn.

6 From the back, bring the threaded needle through to the front at the centre point between two spokes.

7 Take the yarn back over the previous spoke and under the same spoke and the following one.

8 Repeat Step 7 over and over until all spokes have been sewn over row after row and there is no open space at the centre of the ring. Thread the needle through to the reverse of the work and fasten off. To prevent yarns unravelling you can add a dab of glue to the reverse side of the button. Leave one yarn end for sewing to your fabric.

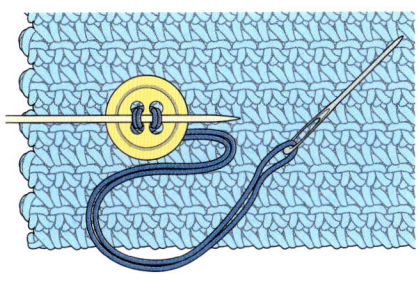

Sewing on a button

It is always a good idea to leave a little 'wiggle room' between the button and the crochet fabric to prevent wear. When sewing the button into place, hold something that will help create space on top of the button as you sew. A **tapestry** needle or a bamboo skewer are good examples of the kind of thing you can use.

Pompoms, fringes and tassels

These sew-on trims add the personal touch that makes any crochet project unique. Use them in any way you choose to decorate your crochet.

Pompoms

Many of us will have made pompoms as children. They are traditionally made using two pieces of circular card, each with a hole cut from the centre so that they are doughnutlike in appearance.

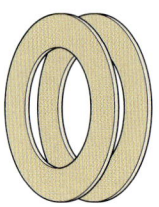
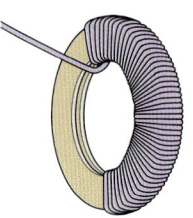
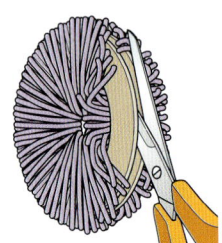

1 Hold the two pieces of card together so that they line up.

2 Wrap the yarn around the circumference of the ring until you can no longer fit any more yarn around it.

3 Cut the yarn in line with the gap between the two pieces of card.

4 Once you have cut the whole way around, tie another yarn end between the two pieces of card and thus also around the cut yarn, and knot tightly. Remove the circular card pieces, fluff up the pompom and trim to shape.

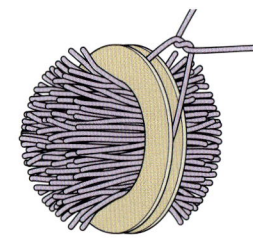

Jane says

Pompoms are so beautifully tactile and are a lot of fun to make. They are brilliant for using up leftover yarns and look great made in lots of different sizes and colours. You can create some interesting effects by wrapping yarn shades in various ways. Look online for some great ideas for making heart pompoms, animal faces and so on.

SEE ALSO

Common Pattern Abbreviations, page 138
Crochet Stitches, pages 38–44

POMPOM VARIETY
You can make pompoms in one shade of yarn or multicoloured. They look great when worked using a combination of yarn thicknesses in a group of colours.

Curly fringe

This is a lovely edging that is especially nice when worked in a relatively light yarn, such as mohair. You can make the length of chains that make up this fringe as long as you want.

Join the yarn into the first st by making 1 ch (does not count as a st), 1 dc into same st, * ch 13, working back along ch just made miss 3 ch, 3 tr into each next 10 ch, miss next st on edge, 1 dc into next st; repeat from * to end.

Chain fringe

Create a series of chain loops to make a fringe of any length.

Join the yarn into the first st by making 1 ch (does not count as a st), 1 dc into same st, [ch 11, 1 dc into next st] to end.

Knotted fringe

You can make a simple yet highly effective fringe by threading short lengths of yarn through the edge stitches of your crochet fabric. The yarn is threaded through in a way that creates a loop, through which the tail ends of yarn are passed and tightened.

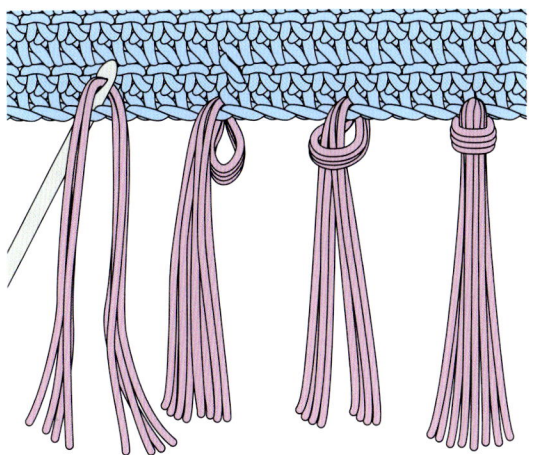

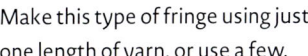
Make this type of fringe using just one length of yarn, or use a few.

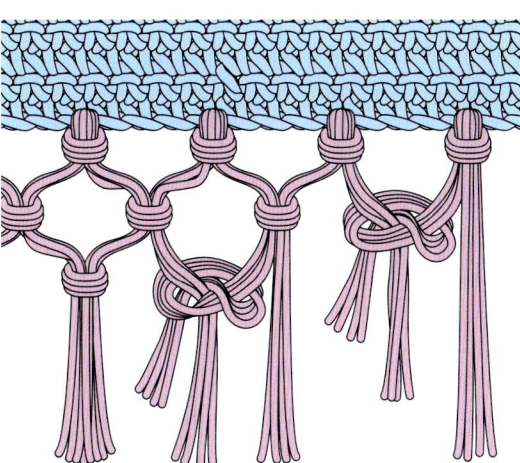
Knot them together in different ways to create alternative effects.

Tassels

You can make separate tassels and use them to decorate the edges of your crochet.

MULTICOLOURED
You could make tassels using yarn scraps from the main project.

1 Cut a piece of card to the length you would like the tassel to be. Wrap the yarn around the card to the required thickness.

2 Knot another length of yarn around the wrapped yarn at the top edge of the card. Do not cut the yarn ends short since you can use them to sew on your tassels later.

3 Take out the card. Knot another yarn around the whole of the tassel towards the top.

4 Wrap this yarn around the tassel as many times as you wish depending on the effect you want to achieve.

5 Using a sharp pair of scissors, cut through the bottom loops of the tassel. Comb through with your fingers and trim to neaten.

Decorative flowers

To design your own flowers, or any other unusual shape, you need to do some calculations before you start. You could choose to make a framework using areas of chain, which are made on one round and then filled up with stitches on the next round to create petals, or you could choose to work directly into stitches.

If you choose to fill up a chain space made on a previous row, the same formula tends to apply as for the first round of a motif: the number of stitches worked into the chain space tends to be (more or less) double the number of chains.

When making petals you need to think about the shape you want to achieve. You may want rounded petals or pointed petals – or a mix of the two. Either way you need to think about the height of the posts of the various stitches you choose to use. I often draw myself a chart to get an idea of a petal shape and tend to work a test on a scrap piece.

Here are some of my patterns to get you practising stitching crochet flowers.

Springtime

Note: All rounds are RS facing. Using first choice of yarn make 4 ch, join with a ss to form a ring.
Foundation round: 1 ch (does not count as a st), 10 dc into ring, ss to join (10 sts).
Round 1: 1 ch (does not count as a st), [1 dc into next st, 2 ch, miss next st,] to end, ss to join, fasten off (5 sts & 5 ch-sps).

Round 2: using second choice of yarn join yarn into any ch-sp by working 1 ch (does not count as a st), [1 dc, 1 htr, 3 tr, 1 htr, 1 dc] into same ch-sp, [1 dc, 1 htr, 3 tr, 1 htr, 1 dc] into each ch-sp to end, ss to join, fasten off (35 sts – 5 petals made).
Sew in yarn ends.

SEE ALSO
Common Pattern Abbreviations, page 138
Crochet Stitches, pages 38–44

Heart rose

Using first choice of yarn make 5 ch, join with a ss to form a ring.

Foundation round: 1 ch (does not count as a st), 12 dc into ring, ss to join, fasten off (12 sts).

Round 1: using second choice of yarn join yarn into any st by working 1 ch + 2 ch (counts as first tr of popcorn), MP into same st, 3 ch, miss next st, *MP into next st, 3 ch, miss next st; repeat from * to end, ss to join, fasten off (6 popcorns made).

Round 2: using third choice of yarn join yarn into any 3 ch-sp by

working 1 ch + 2 ch (counts as 1 tr), 5 tr into same ch-sp, 6 tr into each ch-sp to end, ss to join, fasten off (36 sts).

Round 3: using fourth choice of yarn join yarn into second tr of any 6-tr group made on previous round by working 1 ch + 1 ch (counts as 1 htr), *2 tr into each next 3 sts, 1 htr into next st, 1 ch, miss next st, 1 htr into next st; repeat from * to end, omitting 1 htr on final pattern repeat, ss to second ch of 2-ch at beginning of round to join, fasten off (48 sts).

Round 4: Using third choice of yarn (same shade as round 2) join yarn into st-sp between any 2 groups of 6 tr made on round 2 (also worked using this shade) by working 1 ch (counts as 1SP dc – be careful not to overpull this stitch as it could come loose), *miss ch made on previous round (this is now covered by the SP dc), miss st at top of next htr, [1 dc & 1 htr] into next st, 3 tr into next st, 1 htr into next st, ss into next st, 1 htr into next st, 3 tr into next st, [1 htr & 1 dc] into next st, 1SP dc into st-sp made between next 2 groups of 6 tr made on round 2; repeat from * to end, omitting last SP dc on final pattern repeat, miss SP dc, ss into next st to join, fasten off (84 sts).

Round 5: Using fifth choice of yarn and working at the reverse side of the flower (but with RS facing), join yarn around the reverse side of any SP dc made on previous round by working 1 ch (does not count

as a st), 1 dc into same st, *4 ch, 1 dtr into dc at base of ch-4, 4 ch, ss into same dc, 7 ch, 1 dc into reverse side of next SP dc as before; repeat from * to end, omitting last dc on final pattern repeat, ss to join, fasten off (base for 6 leaves complete).

Round 6: using final choice of yarn join yarn into fourth ch of any 7 ch made on previous round by working 1 ch (does not count as a st), 1 dc into same ch, *1 ch, 1 tr into next ch-sp (between 4 ch & dtr), 1 ch, [1 tr, 1 ch into same ch-sp] three times, 1 tr into same ch-sp, 3 ch, ss into st at base of 3-ch to make picot, [1 tr into next ch sp, 1 ch] five times, miss 3 ch of ch-7 made on previous round, 1 dc into next ch; repeat from * to end, omitting last dc on final pattern repeat, ss to join, fasten off (6 leaves complete). Sew in yarn ends.

Leilani

Note: All rounds are RS facing.
Using first choice of yarn make 5 ch, join with a ss to form a ring.

Round 1: 1 ch (does not count as a st), 12 dc into ring, ss to join (12 sts).

Round 2: 5 ch (counts as 1 tr & 2 ch), [1 tr into next st, 2 ch] to end, ss to join, fasten off (12 tr & 12 ch-sps).

Round 3: using second choice of yarn join yarn into any ch-sp by working 1 ch (does not count as a st), 3 dc into same ch-sp, 3 dc into each ch-sp to end, ss to join, fasten off (36 sts).

Round 4: using third choice of yarn join yarn into any st in line with tr made on round 2 by working 1 ch (does not

count as a st), 1 dc into same st, *1 htr into next st, 2 tr into next st, 1 dtr into next st, 2 tr into next st, 1 htr into next st, 1 dc into next st; repeat from * to end, omitting last dc on final pattern repeat, ss to join, fasten off (48 sts – 6 petals made).

Round 5: using fourth choice of yarn join yarn into dc made between any 2 petals by working 1 ch (does not count as a st), 1 dc into same st, *1 dc into next st, [2 dc into next st] twice, 1 dc into next st, [2 dc into next st] twice, 1 dc into next st, 1 dc into each next 2 sts; repeat from * to end, omitting last dc on final pattern repeat, ss to join, fasten off (72 sts).

Round 6: using final choice of yarn join yarn into st-sp made on round 3 in line with tr made on round 2 by working 1 ch and drawing the yarn up to create a yarn loop around work so far (counts as 1 SP dc), *miss st under SP dc, [1 dc into next st, 1 ch] ten times, 1 dc into next st, 1 SP dc into st-sp made on round 3 in line with next tr made on round 2; repeat from * to end, omitting last tr on final pattern repeat, miss SP dc made at beginning of round, ss to next st to join, fasten off (72 sts & 60 ch-sps).

Sew in yarn ends.

Small rose

Using first choice of yarn make 4 ch, join with a ss to form a ring.

Foundation round: 1 ch (does not count as a st), 12 dc into ring, ss to join (12 sts).

Round 1: 1 ch (does not count as a st), [1 dc into next st, 2 ch, miss next st,] to end, ss to join, fasten off (6 sts & 6 ch-sps).

Round 2: using second choice of yarn join yarn into any ch-sp by working 1 ch + 2 ch (counts as 1 tr), 4 tr into same ch-sp, 1 ch, [5 tr into next ch-sp, 1 ch] to end, ss to join, fasten off (30 sts & 6 ch-sps).

Round 3: using third choice of yarn join yarn into first st of any 5-tr group by working 1 ch (does not count as a st), 1 dc into same st, * [2 tr, 1 htr] into next st, ss into next st, [1 htr, 2 tr] into next st, 1 dc into next st, 1 tr around BP of next dc made on Round 1, miss 1 ch-sp, 1 dc into next st; repeat from * to end omitting 1 dc on final repeat, ss to join, fasten off (60 sts). Sew in yarn ends.

Columbine

Using first choice of yarn make 4 ch, join with a ss to form a ring.

Foundation round: 1 ch (does not count as a st), 8 dc into ring, ss to join, fasten off (8 sts).

Round 1: using second choice of yarn join yarn into any st by working 1 ch (does not count as a st), 2 dc into same st, 2 dc into each st to end, ss to join, fasten off (16 sts).

Round 2: using third choice of yarn join yarn into any st by working 1 ch (does not count as a st), 1 dc into same st, *2 ch, miss next st, 1 dc into next st; repeat from * to end, omitting 1 dc on final pattern repeat, ss to join (8 sts & 8 ch-sps)

Round 3: ss into next ch-sp, 1 ch (does not count as a st), [1 dc, 3 tr, 1 dc] into same ch-sp, [1 dc, 3 tr, 1 dc] into each ch-sp to end, ss to join, fasten off (40 sts – 8 petals made).

Round 4: using fourth choice of yarn and working behind previous round join yarn into any missed

st made on round 1 by working 1 ch (does not count as a st), 1 dc into same st, *2 ch, 1 dc into next missed st; repeat from * omitting 1 dc on final pattern repeat, ss to join (8 sts & 8 ch-sps).

Round 5: ss into next ch-sp, 1 ch (does not count as a st), 1 dc into same ch-sp, * 6 ch, working back along 6 ch just made, miss next ch, 1 dc into next ch, 1 htr into next ch, 1 tr into each next 2 ch, 1 htr into next ch, 1 dc into same ch-sp at base of 6-ch, 1 ch, 1 dc into next ch-sp; repeat from * to end, omitting 1 dc on final pattern repeat, ss to join, fasten off (16 sts & 8 ch-sps – 8 thin leaves made). Sew in yarn ends.

Gillow

Using first choice of yarn make 4 ch, join with a ss to form a ring.

Foundation round: 1 ch (does not count as a st), 8 dc into ring, ss to join, fasten off (8 sts).

Round 1: using second choice of yarn join yarn into any st by working 1 ch + 2 ch (counts as 1 tr), 2 tr into same st, 3 tr into each st to end, ss to join, fasten off (24 sts).

Round 2: using third choice of yarn join yarn into any st by working 1 ch (does not count as a st), 1 dc into same st, 1 ch, [1 dc into next st, 1 ch] to end, ss to join, fasten off (24 sts & 24 ch-sps).

Note: Don't worry if your work is a little wavy at this point.

Round 3: using fourth choice of yarn join yarn into any ch-sp by working 1 ch + 2 ch (counts as 1 tr), 1 tr into same ch-sp, *3 tr into next ch-sp, 1 ch, miss next ch-sp, 2 tr into next ch-sp; repeat from * to end omitting 2 tr on final repeat, ss to join, fasten off (40 sts & 8 ch-sps).

Round 4: using fifth choice of yarn join yarn into first tr of any 5-st group by working 1 ch + 1 ch (counts as 2 ch) *1 tr into next st, 3 ch, ss into st at base of 3-ch to make picot, 2 tr into next st, 3 ch, ss into st at base of 3 ch to make picot, 1 tr into same st, 1 tr into next st, 3 ch, ss into st at base of 3-ch to make picot, 2 ch, ss into next st, 1 ch, miss next ch-sp, ss into next st, 2 ch; repeat from * to end omitting 2 ch on final repeat, ss to join, fasten off (8 ch-sps – 8 petals made each with 3 picots).

Round 5: using sixth choice of yarn and working behind the flower but with RS facing join yarn into any missed ch-sp made on round 2 by working 1 ch (does not count as a st), 1 dc into same ch-sp, [4 ch behind next petal, 1 dc into next ch-sp] seven times, 1 ch, 1 tr into dc made at beginning of round to join (counts as ch-sp), this leaves hook in correct position for next round (8 sts & 8 ch-sps).

Round 6: 1 ch (does not count as a st), 1 dc into ch-sp (made by tr) at base of 1-ch (this is the post of the tr made at end of last round), *3 ch, working in front of ch-sps made between petals 1 tr into next st (this is the dc made on previous round) making sure not to trap 1 ch-sps into st, 3 ch behind next petal, 1 dc into next ch-sp; repeat from * to end omitting 1 dc on final repeat, ss to join, fasten off (8 dc, 8 tr &16 ch-sps).

Sew in yarn ends.

Finishing touches

A PROFESSIONAL FINISH WILL MAKE ALL THE DIFFERENCE
TO YOUR CROCHET PROJECT. WHILE NOT AS INSPIRING
AS CREATING CROCHET FABRICS, A NEAT AND
SKILLFUL FINISH (HOWEVER LONG IT TAKES TO
MAKE) WILL GIVE YOU MORE JOY IN THE LONG
RUN THAN A BAD ONE.

Yarn ends

It is a good idea to sew or weave in your yarn ends as you go along, rather than leaving this process to the end of a project.

Sewing in

Crochet stitches create a clamp around the chain made at the top of previous rows. The space at the base of the post of a stitch creates the perfect tunnel through which you can sew in your yarn ends.

Use a tapestry needle with a large eye and leave the tail ends of the yarn relatively long, so that you can easily thread them through the needle and have enough slack to work your stitches easily.

Sew the tail end of the yarn forward through the tunnel created by stitches for a few stitches, then sew back on yourself every now and again. You can think of this as three or four steps forward, then one step back. Try not to sew too tightly, and pull slightly to relieve the tension every now and again.

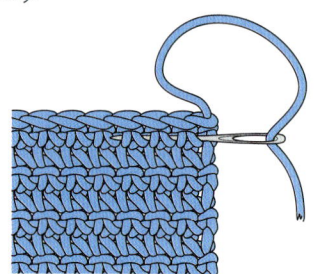

Jane says

As crocheters we love the process of creating fabrics with yarn and a hook, but it can be difficult to feel as inspired by the finishing process. To help make this a less painful task, try breaking it up into bitesize pieces. For example, sew or weave yarn ends in as you go along, rather than leaving this job until the end of the project.

When making garments, do some of the seaming (see pages 135–136) as you complete the crochet pieces. For example, you can join the back and front pieces by creating the shoulder seams and add the button band or neckline before making the sleeves.

Try to embrace the process and think of it as part of your cherished craft time.

Weaving in as you crochet

You can weave ends in as you crochet so that you don't have to sew them in. This works best when working stitches with short posts, such as double crochet or half treble crochet.

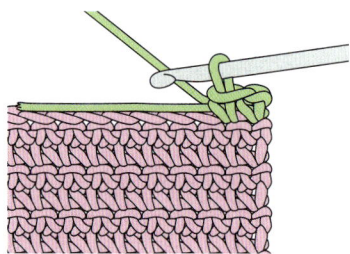

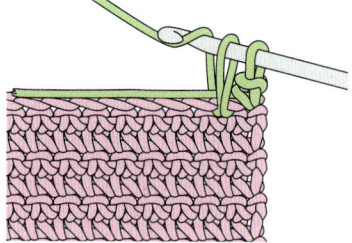

1 Hold the tail end of yarn (the one you want to weave in) horizontally in line with the top of your work so that it lines up with the chain at the top of the stitches.

2 Work the next row of crochet over the yarn tail to trap it into the tunnel made at the base of the stitches. It is a good idea to do this for ten stitches or more since short tails can work their way loose. Pull the tension back slightly before trimming the yarn ends.

Blocking

Blocking is the process of laying out individual crochet pieces before joining them together, then either steaming or moistening them with water to slightly stretch them and relax the yarn.

You will have put a lot of time and effort into creating your crochet elements in order to produce a beautiful handmade piece, so it is also worth taking plenty of time to make sure that all the pieces are finished in the nicest way possible.

Blocking board

A blocking board can be as simple or as elaborate as you want it to be. You can buy special foam jigsaw blocking mats, or pick virtually the same things up at a toy store at a fraction of the cost. You can also use the top of an ironing board or a bath towel on the floor.

Pin out your pieces

When blocking out a flat piece, lay it on a clean kitchen or bath towel. A striped or checked towel is a good choice to help with lining up and measuring.

To block three-dimensional pieces, lay them the right way up so that you can see all the elements.

Pin your crochet pieces in place, using a ruler to ensure you are blocking to the right size. Only very slightly stretch the piece, and put the pins in as flat as you can.

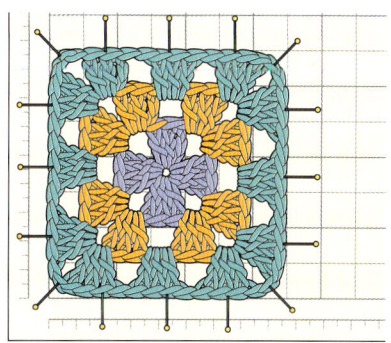

Jane says

When I'm pinning out a large project I work from the centre out, marking the central point of each side first, then working towards each corner.

Jane says

Crochet pieces love to curl up, so there is no point blocking each crochet motif as you complete it because by the time you come to join your pieces together they will have curled up again and will need reblocking.

Using steam

If you have a steam iron that you know you can trust, and that can produce steam without spurting boiling water, you can steam your crochet pieces, but be sure to hold the iron a few inches above your crochet to ensure it doesn't get too hot.

Using a water spray

You can also use a spray bottle, such as a plant mister, filled with clean, cold water. Spray until the pieces are nicely damp, but not soaking. Once the yarn has taken in the water, leave the pieces to dry completely before removing the pins.

Joining blocks

You can either use crochet stitches to join your pieces together, or make sewn stitches. Most crocheters opt to crochet since they find it far easier and quicker. The methods included here create slightly different effects, and will use varying amounts of yarn.

In the step sequences here we have used a contrasting yarn shade to clearly differentiate the yarn used to make the seam from the yarns in the crochet fabric. When putting your own project together, however, you will use a matching yarn shade, so make sure you have enough yarn in the same shade to create your seams.

Jane says

Seams are easiest to join when the crochet pieces have the same stitch count. If you are joining pieces that are not identical you can use markers or pins to line things up. When joining a big project, it is a good idea to work out the best route for your stitching so that there are not too many yarn joins.

SEE ALSO

Backstitch, page 113
Borders and Edgings, pages 106–110
Crochet Stitches, pages 38–44
Traditional Granny Square, page 70

Double crochet on the wrong side

This joining method creates a visible flat join that looks a little like stitching between the crochet pieces. It can look particularly effective when worked in an alternative yarn shade.

1 Line the crochet pieces up against each other so that the right sides of the work face inwards.

2 Insert the hook into the first stitch on both pieces so that it is under the chain stitch at the top of the stitches.

3 Wrap the yarn around the hook and draw through the work, making one chain, which does not count as a stitch.

4 Stitch one double crochet into the same pair of stitches.

5 Stitch one double crochet into each matching pair of stitches to the end, then fasten off.

WRONG-SIDE JOIN IN PROGRESS

Jane says

When creating a join on the right side of the work using the double crochet method, the reverse side of the stitches present to the front, meaning that the less neat side of the stitch is more visible. This can look a little messy.

If you want to make this join look neater and at the same time make the seam more of a feature, work double crochet on the right side of the work to join your stitches but do not fasten off the yarn at the end of the join. Instead, change to a larger size hook and work slip stitches back along the join, working into the top of the chain on each of the double crochet stitches.

Double crochet on the right side

Using the double crochet join on the right side of the work will create a more visible, ridged join. Line up the crochet pieces so that the wrong sides of the work are facing inwards, and follow the instructions opposite.

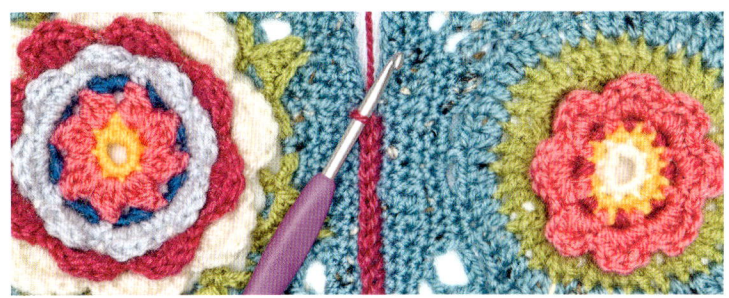

Slip-stitch join

This is a good join to make if you think you might be running a little short of yarn. It creates a similar join to the double crochet join, but is a little tighter and less flat.

Using a size larger hook than the one you made the crochet fabric with, work Steps 1–3 of Double Crochet on the Wrong Side. To continue, work slip stitches into each pair of stitches to the end, then fasten off.

COMPLETED
WRONG-SIDE JOIN

SLIP-STITCH JOIN
IN PROGRESS

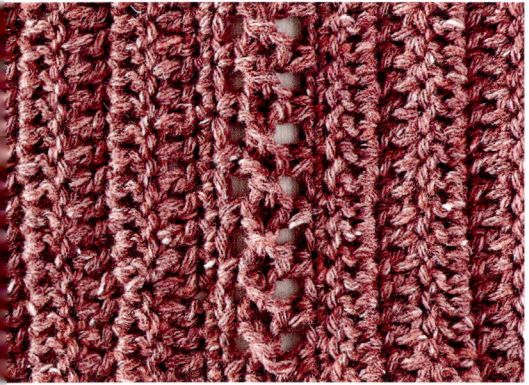

Continuous flat braid join

This decorative join is a little fiddly to make since you need to continuously remove the yarn loop from the hook, but it creates a lovely effect and is a particularly good way of joining crochet fabrics made using double crochet. The method is worked using the join-as-you-go method (see page 134).

Using the joining shade of yarn and making sure that the stitches are evenly spaced, work around the edge of one motif to create a chain and double crochet edging. In this example there are three chains between each double crochet and five chains at the corners.

1 Lay your pieces side by side on a flat surface so that you can clearly see the fabric edges. Place the crochet piece with the edging on the right-hand side. Starting on the left-hand piece, join the yarn into the first stitch space between the two edge stitches of the crochet fabric by working one chain, which does not count as a stitch. Make one double crochet into the same place.

2 Make one chain. Pull the hook a little to make the yarn loop a little bigger, then remove the yarn loop from hook.

3 From the front, insert the hook through the first corresponding chain space on the right-hand piece, and place the yarn loop back on the hook.

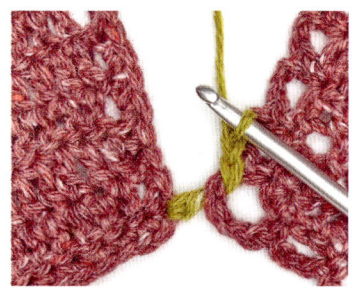

4 Pull the yarn loop though the stitch space. Make two chains and one double crochet into the next stitch space on the left-hand piece.

5 Repeat Steps 2–4 to complete the join.

Chain joins

This is a good method for joining crochet motifs that feature a chain stitch at regular intervals on the final round. This could be one chain between two blocks of treble crochet – as on a granny square – or larger groups of chain stitches.

1 Line the crochet pieces against each other so that the right sides of the work face inwards. Insert the hook into the corner chain space on both blocks.

2 Wrap the yarn around the hook and draw through the chain spaces. Make one chain, which does not count as a stitch, and one double crochet into the same pair of chain spaces.

3 Work the number of chains needed to take you along to the next pair of chain spaces. In this example that is four chains.

4 Make one double crochet into the next pair of chain spaces.

5 Repeat Steps 3–4 to complete the join.

Join as you go

The basic principle of the join-as-you-go method is that you replace a chain stitch with a joining stitch in order to attach two pieces together.

This technique works best when joining motifs worked in the round, and is created while working the final round.

JOINING GRANNY SQUARES AS YOU GO

Make one complete granny square, then make the second granny square up to the beginning of the final round. While crocheting the next side of the motif, join the two together as follows:

1 3 tr into next corner ch-sp, 1 ch, 1 ss into corresponding corner ch-sp on the first motif you made (this replaces the second ch of 3-ch and joins the pieces).

2 1 ch, 3 tr into same ch-sp to create the corner join.

3 Instead of making 1 ch, work 1 dc into next corresponding ch-sp on the first motif to join, 3 tr into next ch-sp.

4 Repeat the last step until you reach the next corner ch-sp. 1 ch, 1 ss into corresponding corner ch-sp on the first motif you made (this replaces the second ch of 3-ch and joins the pieces), 1 ch, 3 tr into same ch-sp. Motifs are joined along one side.

5 Complete the remaining sides of the motif by following the granny-square pattern.

JOINING A CHAIN-EDGED MOTIF AS YOU GO

To use the join-as-you-go method using chain and slip stitch you will need to complete one motif all the way through and then work further motifs to the beginning of the final round (as for the granny square join).

For this example the final round is made by working a repeat of one double crochet and five chains all the way around. To join the motifs, replace the third chain with a slip stitch to join into the corresponding chain space on the completed motif.

Sewing techniques

Many crocheters are not keen on the idea of sewing their blocks together; however, there are times when it can create a neater seam, and can be more economical in terms of yarn use.

Backstitch

Backstitch is a strong sewing stitch for joining seams, but it can create quite a bulky seam. It is worked with the 'inside out', in that you are working with the wrong sides of the work facing, so it is important to keep checking the right sides to ensure you are working in a neat way.

Use a tapestry needle with an eye large enough to take your chosen yarn, and tie a knot in the tail end.

Line the crochet pieces against each other so that the right sides of the work face inwards, and follow the backstitch instructions on page 113. Working through the stitch spaces made between the edge stitches, sew the backstitch one stitch in from the edge of the fabric.

Oversewing

Oversewing can give an effective seam and is probably the most common method crocheters use when sewing pieces together. To create a neat seam it is important to keep your stitch size and spacing consistent.

Use a tapestry needle with an eye large enough to take your chosen yarn, and tie a knot in the tail end.

Line the crochet pieces against each other so that the right sides of the work face inwards. Insert the needle through both fabrics from the back. Draw through to the front, and take the thread around the edge of the work. Insert the needle from the back through the next stitch along, and draw through to the front. Continue working in the same way to complete the required number of stitches, being sure not to overtighten the yarn as you work.

Jane says

When working backstitch along top edges, you can work under the chain at the top of the stitches. When working backstitch along foundation rows, use the remaining part of the chain.

SEE ALSO

Sewn Embellishments, pages 112–114

Mattress stitch

This stitch is particularly effective when used to join double crochet. It produces a neat, straight seam.

1 Lay the crochet pieces side by side on a flat surface. Thread a tapestry needle with a large eye with a length of yarn slightly longer than the length of the seam you want to join, allowing enough yarn to sew the tail end in.

2 Insert the needle from the back through the first stitch space on one piece, and draw through to the front.

3 Insert the needle from the front into the corresponding stitch on the opposite piece. Take the needle up vertically and bring to the front through the stitch on the next row.

4 Insert the needle from the front though the stitch on the opposite piece where the yarn is already leaving from. Take the needle up vertically and bring to the front through the stitch on the next row.

5 Repeat from Step 3, pulling the yarn end to draw the fabric edges together every few stitches, and making sure not to overtighten the yarn.

Washing and storing

Washing a completed piece can make a big difference to its finished appearance. Seams become flatter and stitches become more even, but you need to be careful to protect your hand crochet in the washing process and in storage.

Washing advice

Hand wash items using a liquid detergent, specially formulated for that purpose, and avoid biological liquids or powders since these may contain brighteners that can destroy yarn fibres and cause bobbles and shade changes.

In most cases it is wise to avoid machine washing your crochet. The spin actions on modern machines can be quite destructive to handmade products and, if you put your completed project in with other wash items, they may snag and catch on fastenings or clasps.

Once the piece is washed, place it in a tied pillowcase and give it a short, gentle spin in the washing machine to remove as much water as possible. Throw in a couple of bath towels at the same time to minimize the amount of movement the project will be subject to, and to help absorb water.

Remove the project from the pillowcase and lay it on a bath towel or large, soft, flat surface to dry. Don't place in direct sunlight or over a radiator, and do not tumble dry.

Storage protection

Protect yarns with animal-derived fibre content, such as wool or silk, from destruction by common clothes moths. Moths are attracted to keratin, a fibrous protein that they can feed on. Cotton, polyester and rayon can also be targeted by moths if soiled by food stains or body oils.

Make sure your crochet items are clean before storing. If you are putting items away for a long period of time, wrap them in air-free ziplock bags. Add natural moth deterrents such as a small block of cedarwood, or herbs such as lavender, bay leaves, rosemary thyme, and cloves to the bag to help deter moths. These herbs will also make your project smell nice!

Check your stored items every now and again to ensure they are moth free. At the first sign of moths, such as irregular holes in the fabric, flying moths or eggs, place the item in a freezer for a few hours and the cold will kill the larvae.

If you notice a stain that is still evident after washing, rub it with a vinegar and water solution as this will deter moths too.

Useful information

Over the next few pages you will find extra information you may find useful, from common abbreviations and chart symbols to resources for further learning, connection with other crocheters and stockists of crochet tools and materials.

Common pattern abbreviations

To read and understand a written pattern you need to have a knowledge of the abbreviations for stitches. Most patterns will assume you know basic abbreviations, but may include an explanation for more complex or unusual stitches in an abbreviated form.

Below is a list of common crochet abbreviations, but be aware that abbreviations may vary from one pattern publisher to another, so always read the list provided with the pattern before starting a project.

beg	beginning	**tbl**	through back loop
BO	bobble	**tch**	turning chain
BP	back post	**tfl**	through front loop
bdc	beaded double crochet	**tog**	together
ch	chain	**trtr**	triple treble crochet
CL	cluster	**WS**	wrong side
cdc	crossed double crochet	**yo**	yarn over
tr	treble crochet		
dtr	double treble crochet		**GENERAL INSTRUCTIONS**
FP	front post	*	Start of repeat
htr	half treble crochet	**	End of last repeat
PC	popcorn	[]	Repeat instructions within brackets the stated number of times
PS	puff stitch		
rep	repeat		
RS	right side	( )	Can either be explanatory (counts as 1 tr) or can be read as a group of stitches worked into the same stitch or space (1 dc, 2 ch, 1 dc)
dc	double crochet		
sl st	slip stitch		
sp	space		
spdc	spike double crochet		
st(s)	stitch(es)		

Common chart symbols

Symbols on a chart represent a stitch or instruction, usually detailed on an accompanying key (see page 33).

These are common chart symbols, but always check your particular chart for variations.

magic ring
chain
• slip stitch
+ double crochet
half treble crochet
treble crochet
double treble crochet
triple treble crochet

 cluster (e.g. cluster of 4 tr)
bobble (e.g. bobble of 5 tr)
popcorn (e.g. popcorn of 5 tr)
puff stitch (e.g. puff of 5 htr)
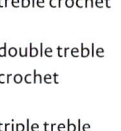 through back loop (e.g. dctbl)
 through front loop (e.g. dctfl)

 front post (e.g. FPtr)
back post (e.g. BPtr)
spike double crochet
♦ beaded double crochet
↗ direction of work

Riders, yankers and lifters

It is quite common for crocheters to achieve close to the correct tension when working stitches with short posts (see The Anatomy of a Stitch, pages 45–47), such as double crochet, only to find they cannot get it right when working stitches with longer posts. This is essentially because the more times the yarn is wrapped around the hook, the more room there is to achieve a slightly different tension on each step of the stitch. The angle at which you hold your hook can also have an impact on the tension of each step of the stitch.

The way crocheters work stitches has recently been divided into three main groups.

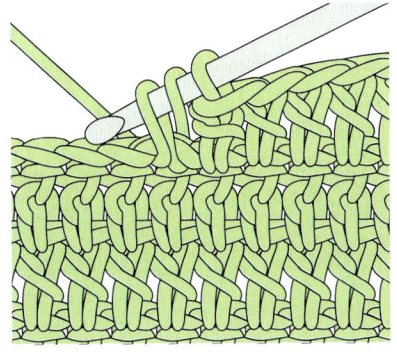

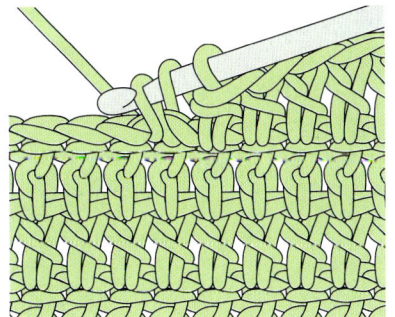

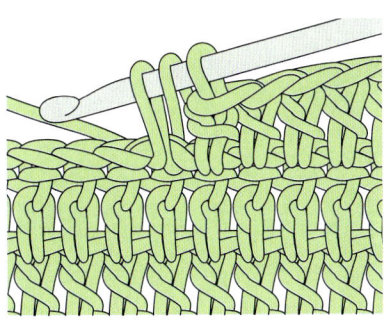

- **RIDERS** A rider is a crocheter who achieves the right height on their stitch post. Riders achieve stitches that are evenly balanced, with each step of the stitch coming out to a similar tension.

- **YANKERS** A yanker overtightens the first step of the stitch. This is often caused by holding the yarn too tightly and by keeping the crochet hook too low when drawing the yarn through the stitch, and therefore not taking the yarn far enough onto the shaft.

- **LIFTERS** A lifter pulls the yarn loop on the hook once it has been drawn through the stitch. Some patterns, such as puff stitches, require you to pull the yarn loop up, but as a rule it should only be lifted to approximately half the height of the stitch.

Resources

JANIE CROW

https://www.janiecrow.com

Instagram
https://www.instagram.com/janiecrow/

Facebook
 https://www.facebook.com/JanieCrowDesign

YouTube
https://www.youtube.com/@janiecrow8472

Pinterest
https://www.pinterest.co.uk/JanieCrow/

CROCHET GUILDS

Knitting and Crochet Guild of Great Britain
https://kcguild.org.uk

YARN BOARDS

Crafts Council
https://www.craftscouncil.org.uk

British Wool
https://www.britishwool.org.uk

Knitting & Crochet Guild
https://kcguild.org.u

PATTERNS, SUPPLIES AND CHAT FORUMS

Crochet Society
https://crochetsociety.co.uk/
Video tutorials, patterns, supplies and more.

Crochetville
https://crochetville.com
Online crochet community

Etsy
https://www.etsy.com
Global marketplace for unique, handcrafted goods

Love Crafts
https://www.lovecrafts.com/en-gb/
Offers a huge collection of different types of yarn with
worldwide shipping

Ravelry
https://www.ravelry.com
Inclusive website for knitters, crocheters, spinners,
weavers, and dyers made up of millions of yarn lovers
from around the world

Stylecraft Yarns
https://stylecraft-yarns.co.uk
Yarns and downloadable patterns

The Crochet Project
https://thecrochetproject.com/
Patterns, tutorials and online classes

Yarnspirations
https://www.yarnspirations.com
Patterns, yarns, tools and online community

Yarnsub
https://www.yarnsub.com
Search engine for substituting yarn for different
crochet pattern and projects

Index

Acknowledgements

I am passionate about the importance of passing on craft knowledge through the generations, and so am incredibly pleased to have had the chance to create *Perfect Crochet Finish*.

I would like to thank the team at Quarto, especially Claire Waite Brown and Martina Calvio who have been so supportive throughout the process of creating this book. With special thanks to Phil Wilkins for his calm and professional approach to the photography and for taking such fantastically clear images.

I am lucky to have the support of Annabelle Hill, Sales and Marketing Director of Stylecraft Yarns, who kindly agreed to provide the lovely yarn used in this book, which include some of their newer natural yarns made from organic cotton, as well as recycled yarns, that are kinder to the planet.

I would like to thank my friend and invaluable assistant Sarah Hazell for all her incredible input into this book. Sarah worked hard to create the crochet samples used for the step-by-step photography and final images in a very tight timescale and I am so grateful to her for the commitment, drive and support she provided to me as we worked through this project. A true and dear friend!

I have worked within the craft industry for many years and am still continuously blessed by the support of crocheters worldwide. My career would not have existed over the last three decades without them, and I am forever indebted to the wonderful crocheters who have been a part of my life. For me, yarn is an addiction and crocheting is like a drug. I can't imagine my life without it and hope that my future will always involve a fix of it. Writing *Perfect Crochet Finish* has been a joy from start to finish and I hope that it will become an invaluable resource to help guide new and experienced crocheters alike.

DEDICATION
For fabulous crocheters and yarn lovers the world over.

PATTERNS AND KITS
Patterns and kits for Jane's designs can be bought at https://www.janiecrow.com/

Designs Jane has used in the book:

Fields of Gold	Mexican Diamonds
Mystical Lanterns	Spirit of Flora
The Fruit Garden	Summer Palace
Lily Pond	

STYLECRAFT YARNS
https://stylecraft-yarns.co.uk
With big thanks to Stylecraft for supporting the yarn used in this book.

LEANNE JADE PHOTOGRAPHY
https://leannejade.com
With big thanks to Leanne for the author and product photographs on pages 7–9, 30 and 73.